I0502742

Nature Mandalas Coloring Book

Copyright: Published in the United States by Nancy McCowan
Published January 2017
ISBN-13: 978-1542630207
ISBN-10: 1542630207

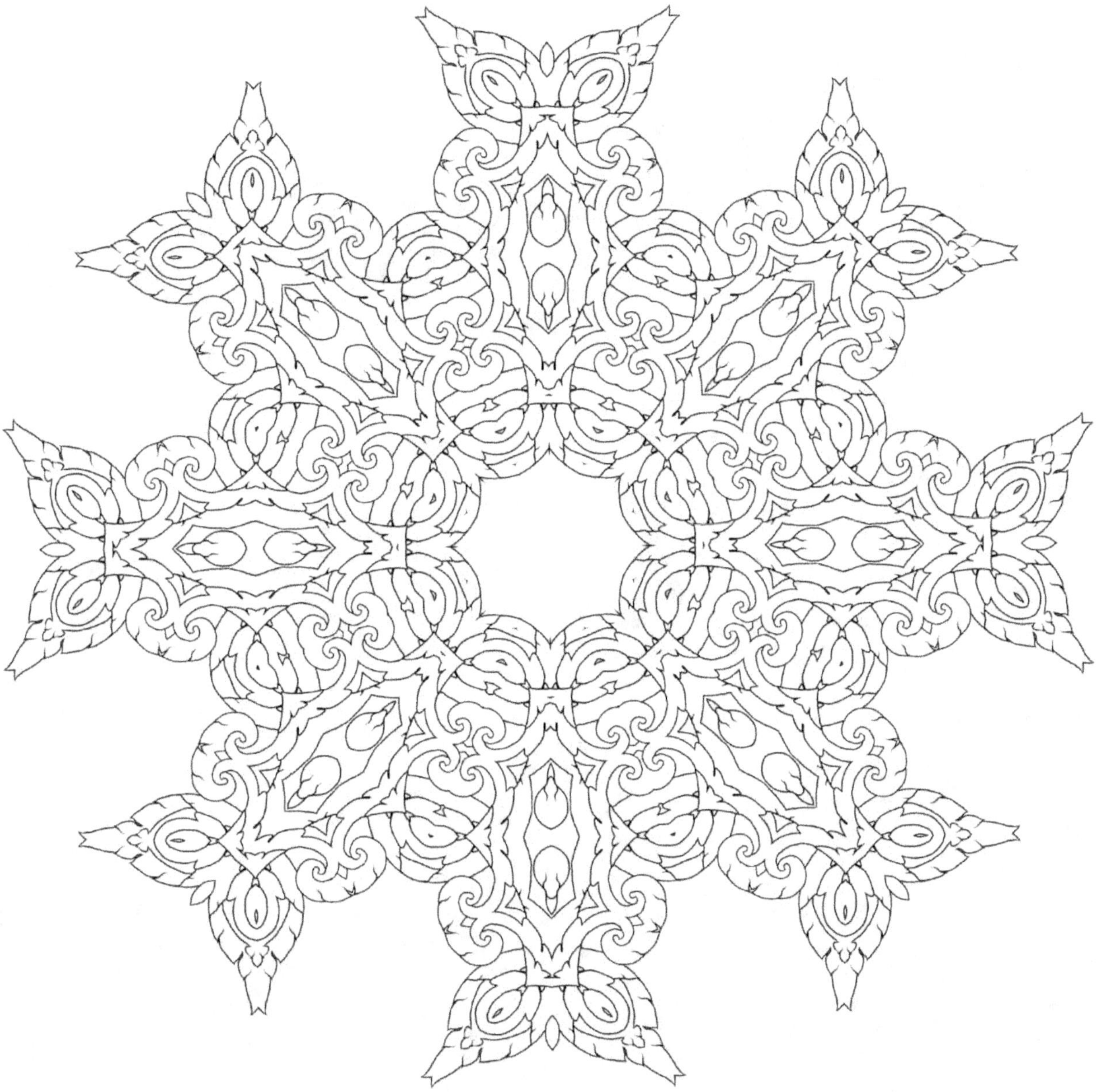

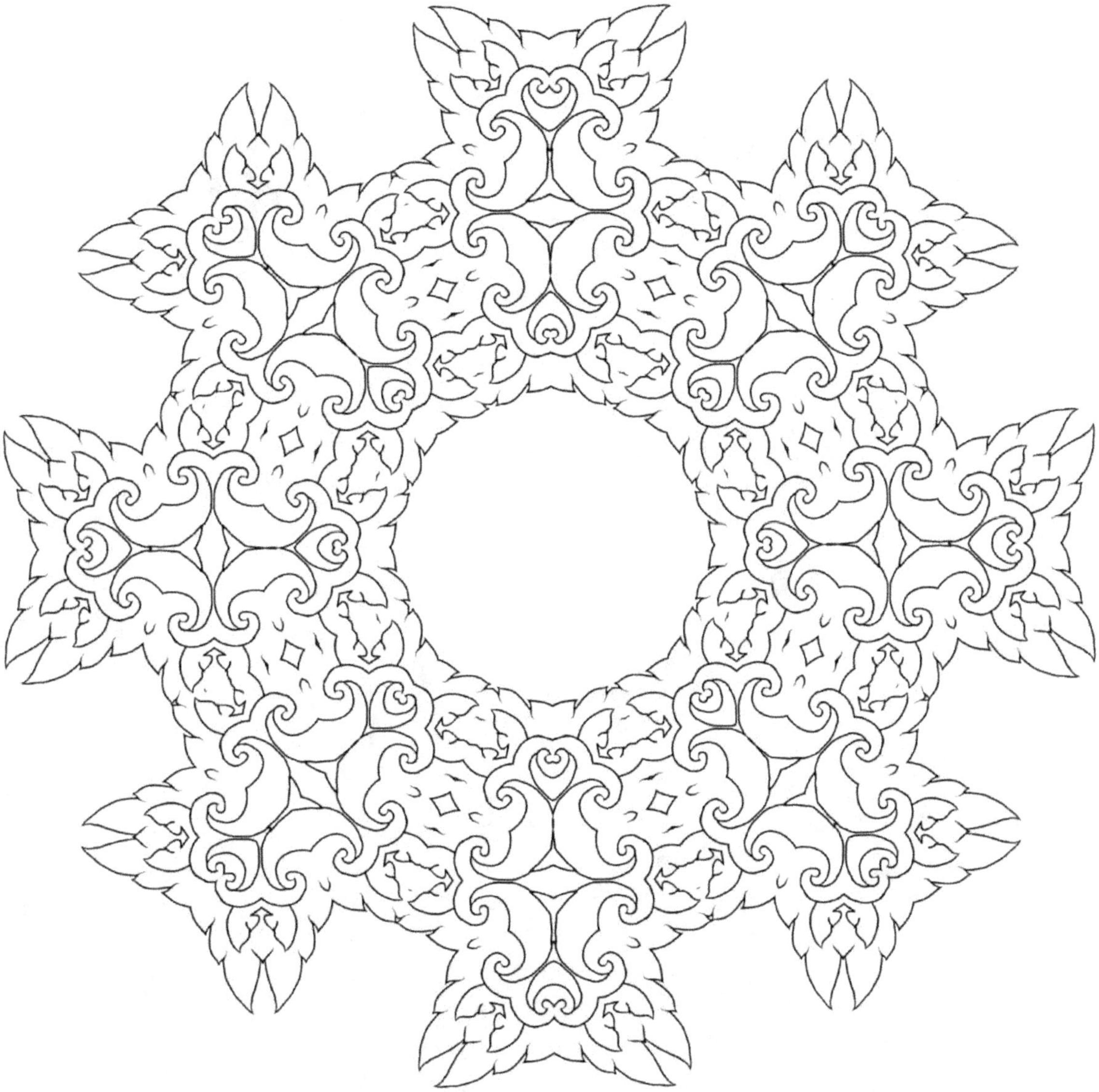

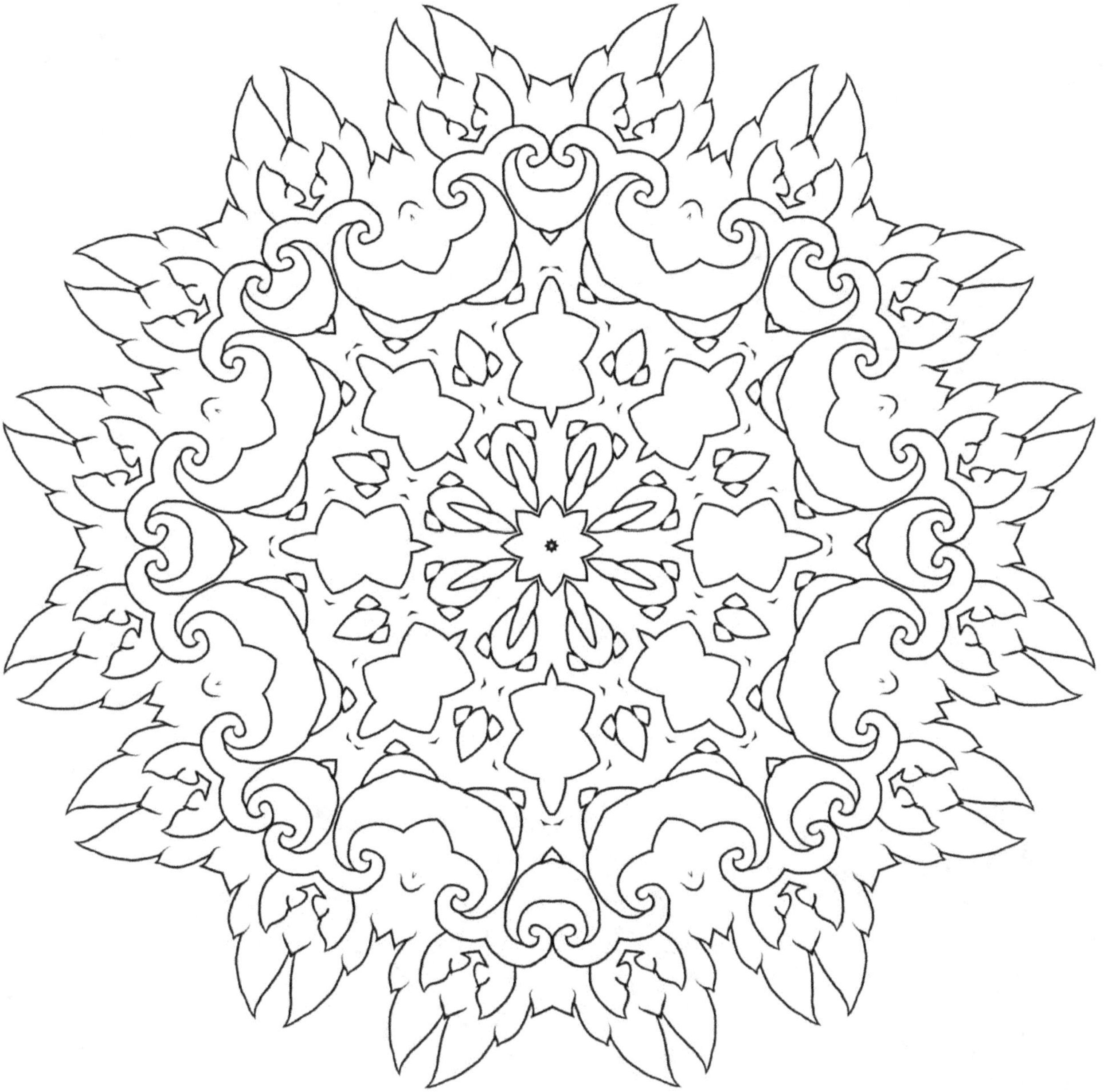

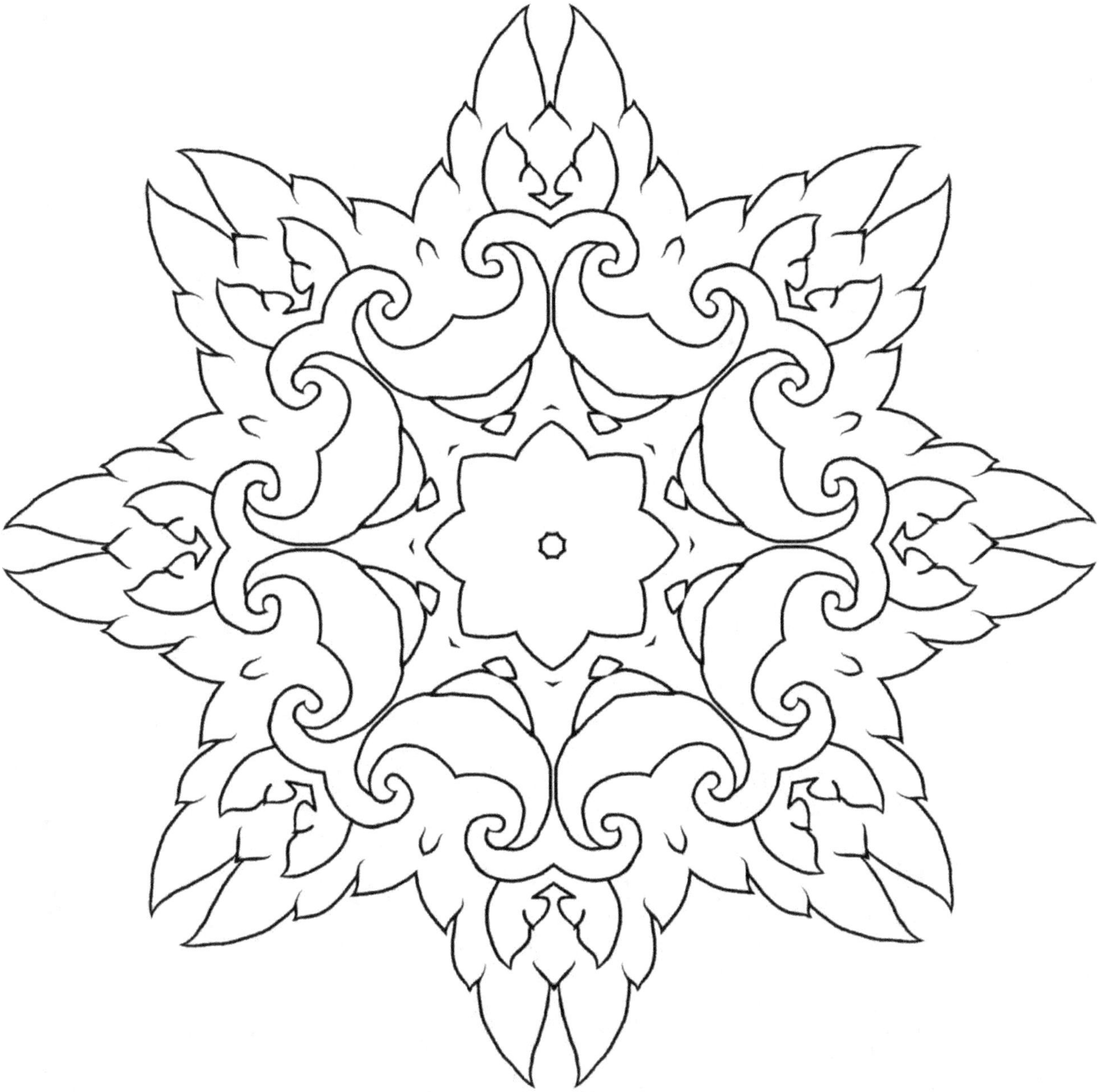

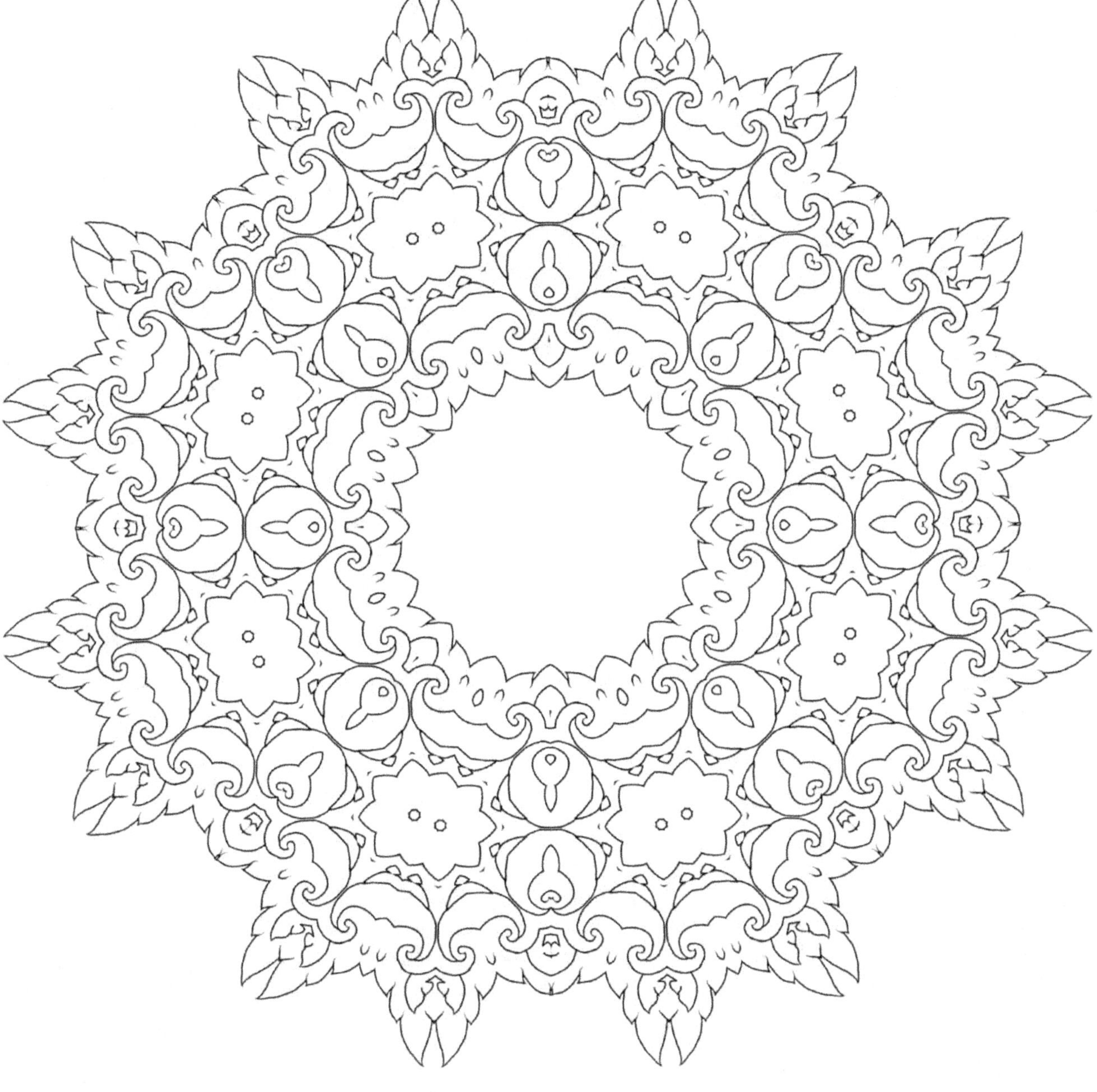

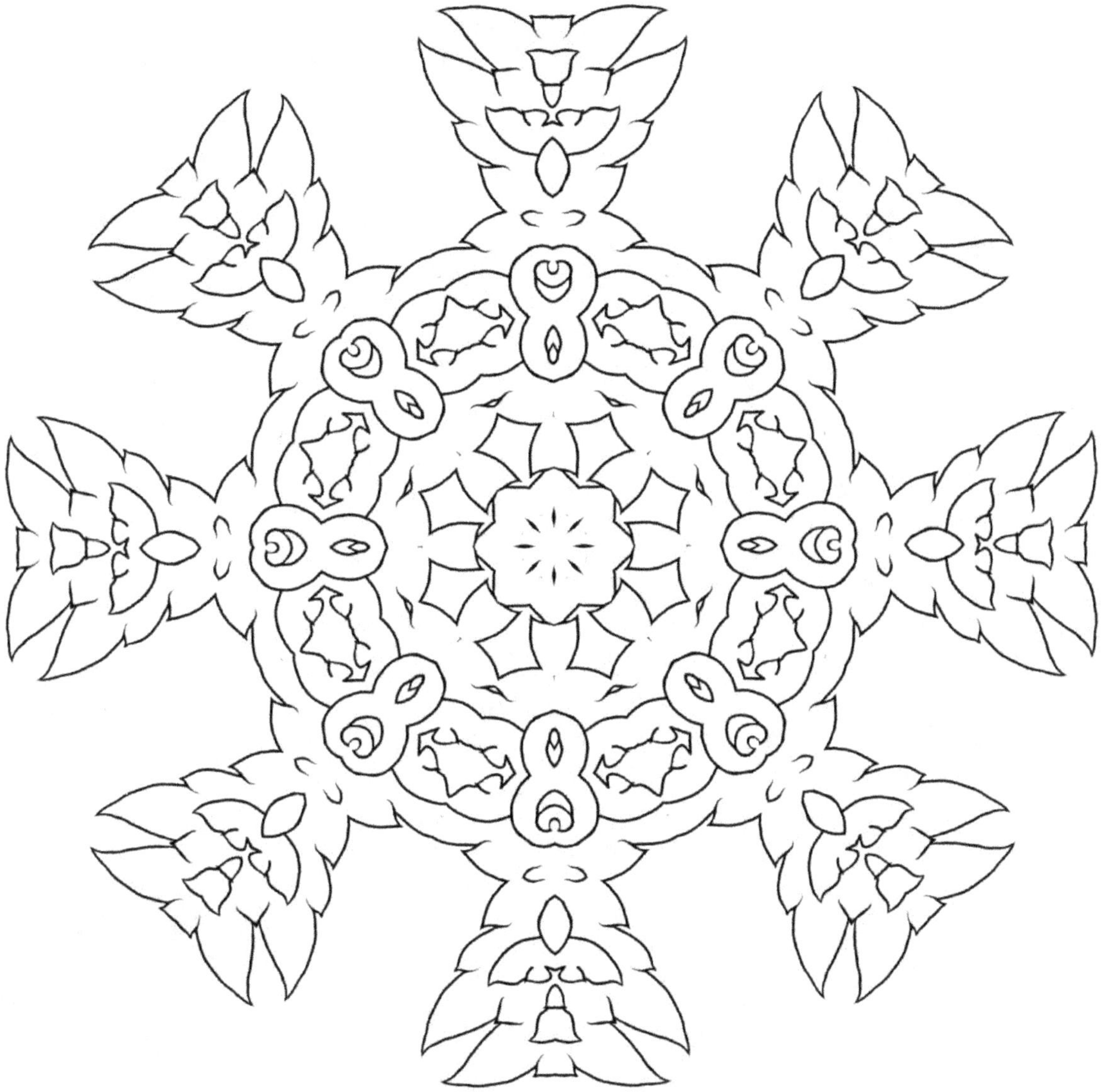

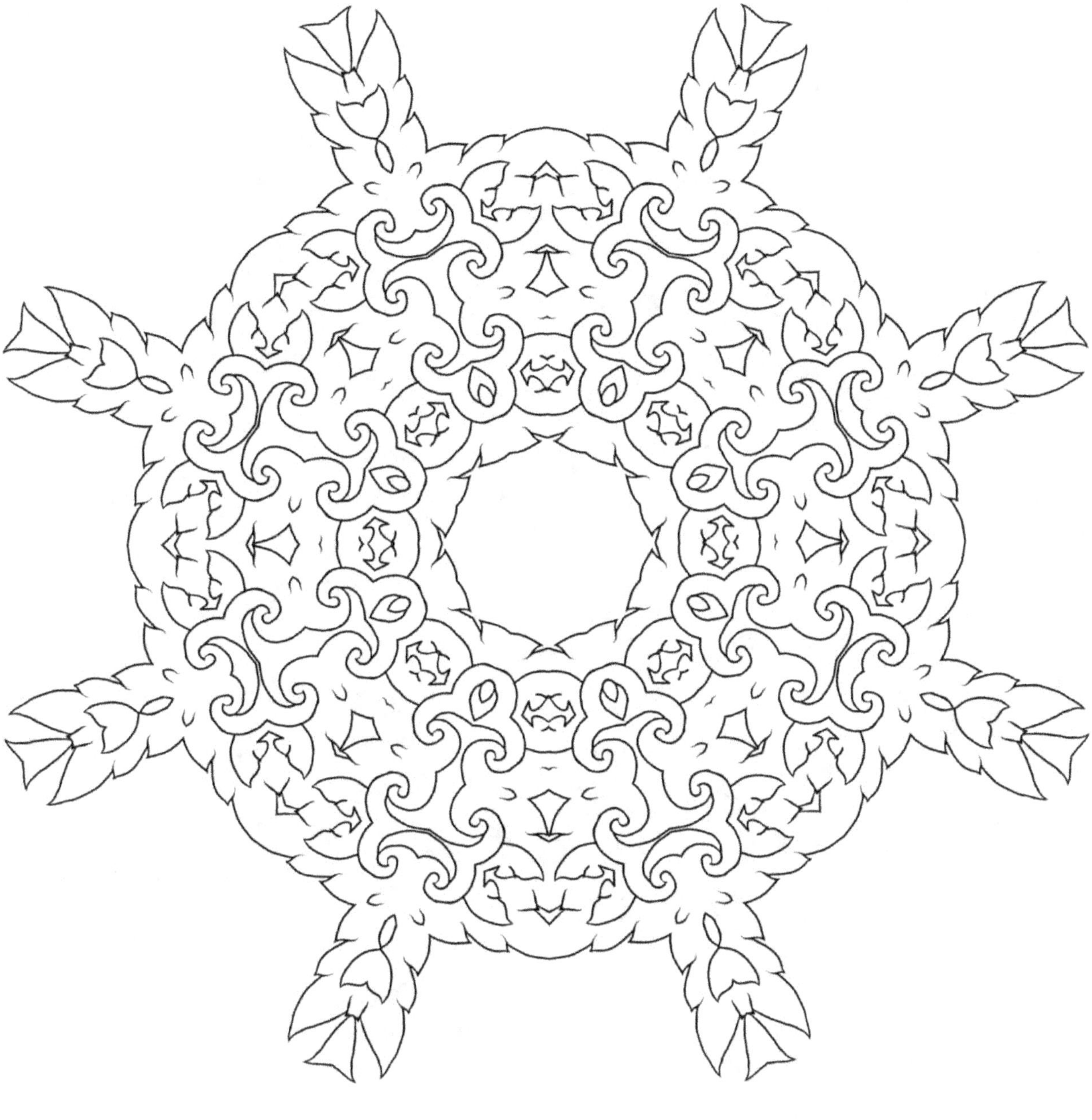

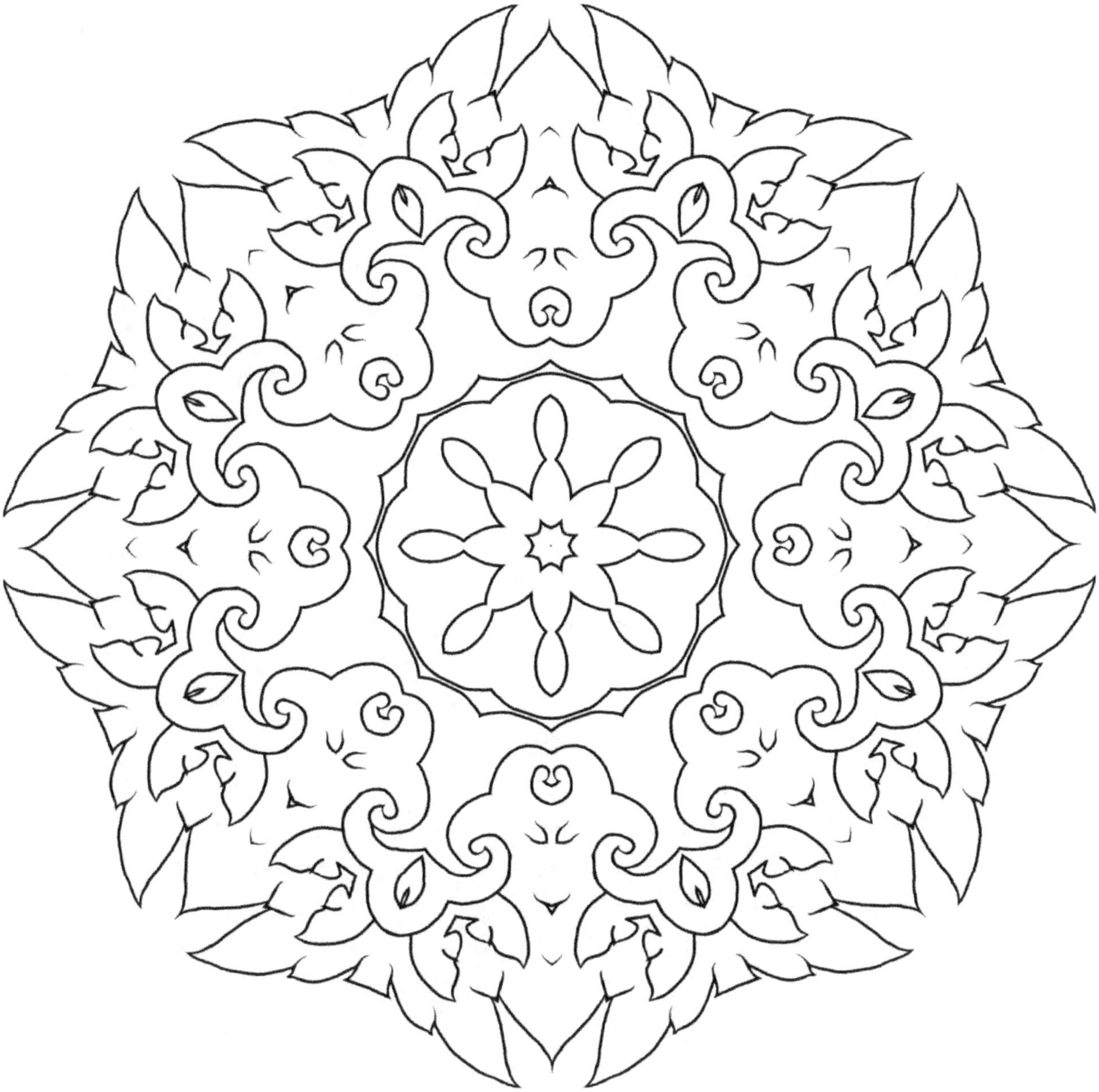

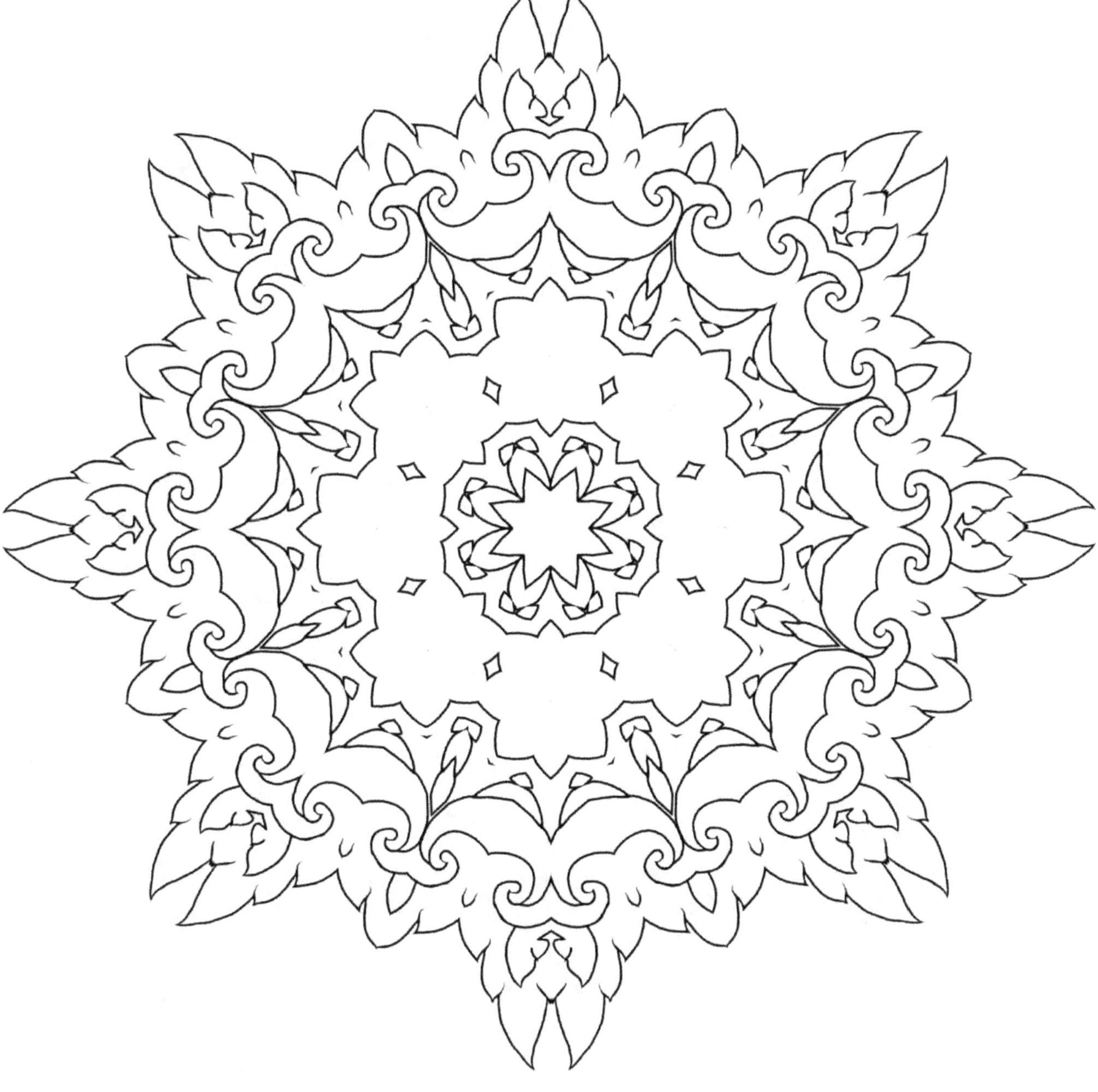

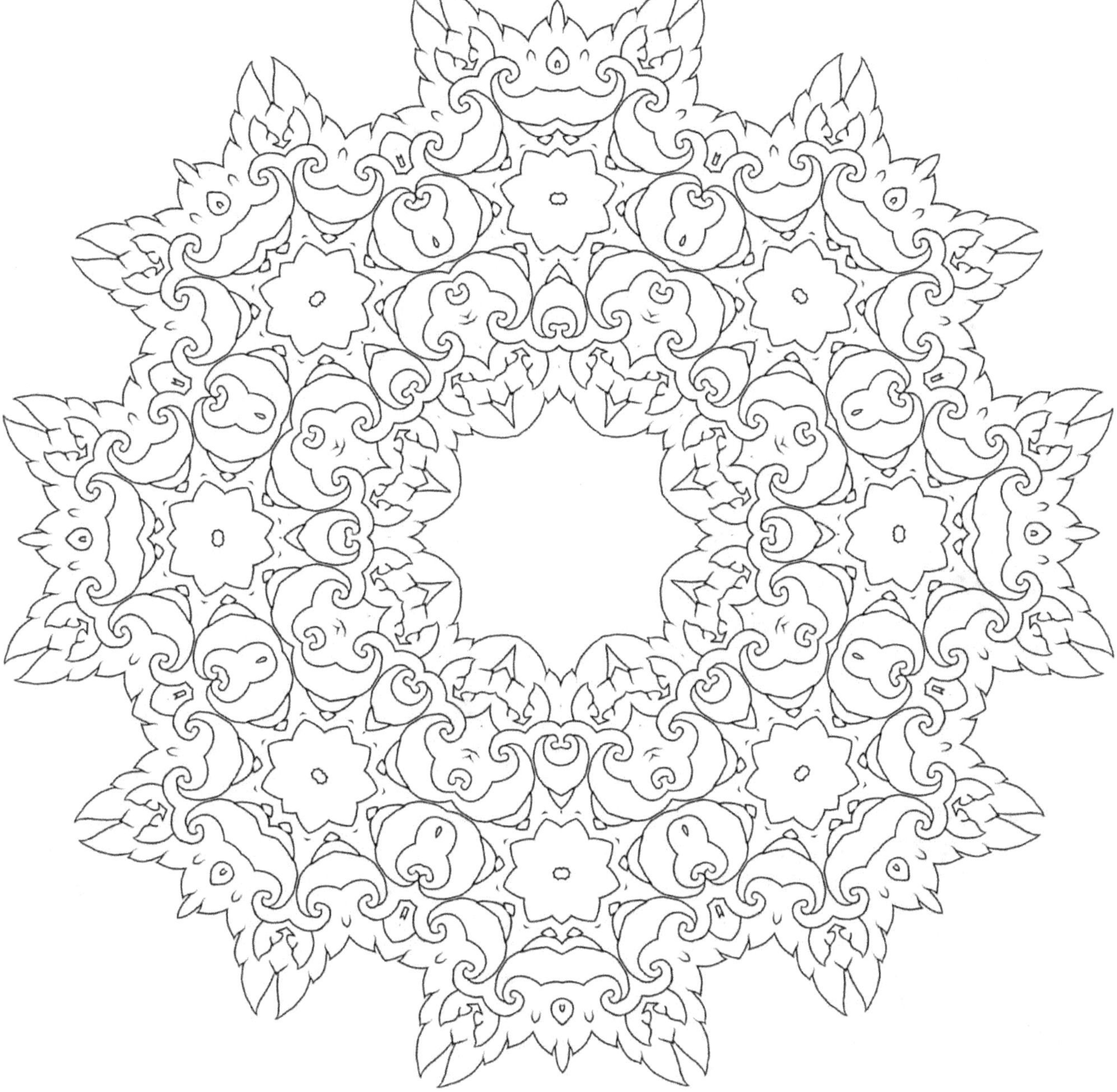

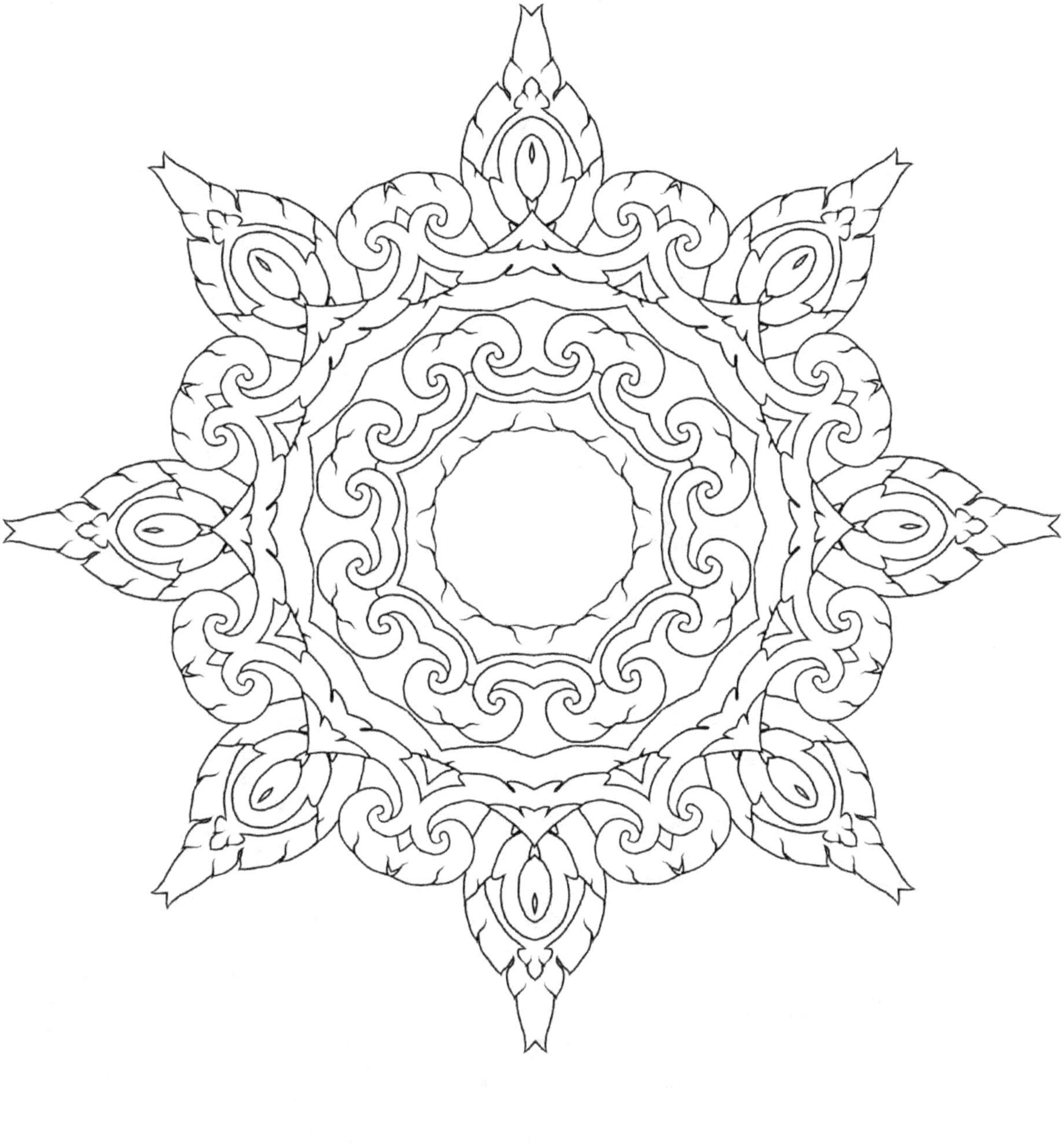

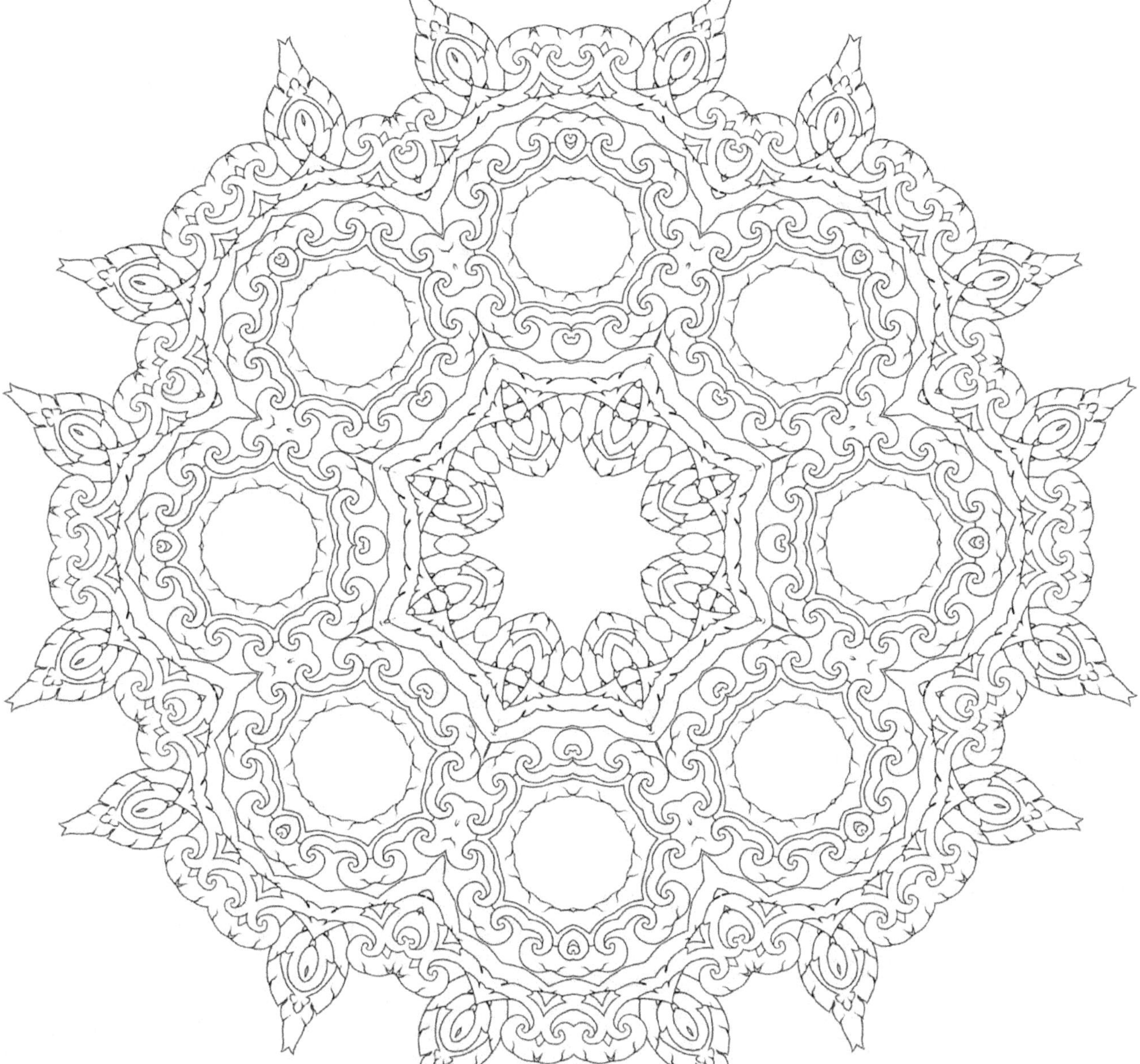

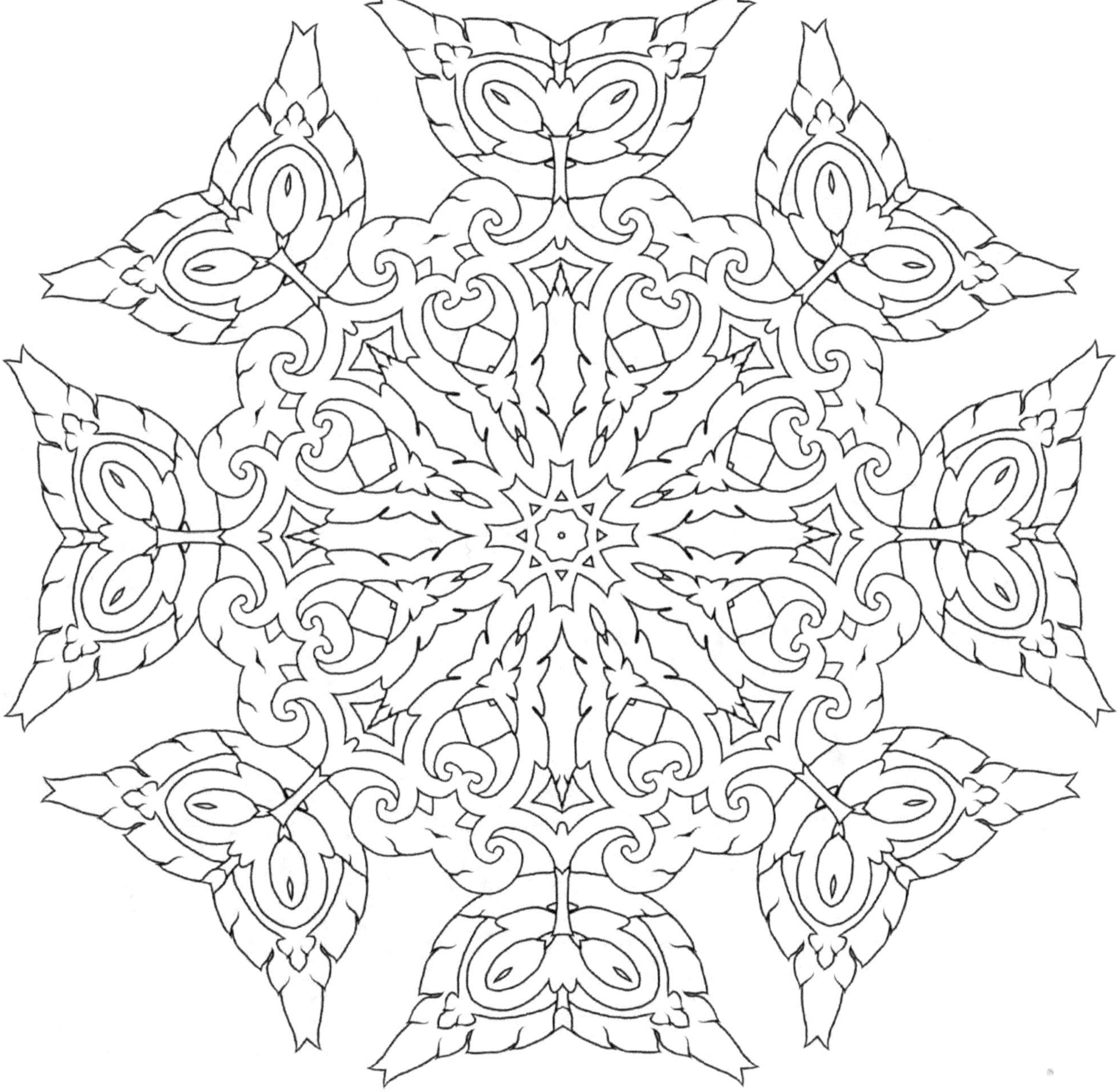

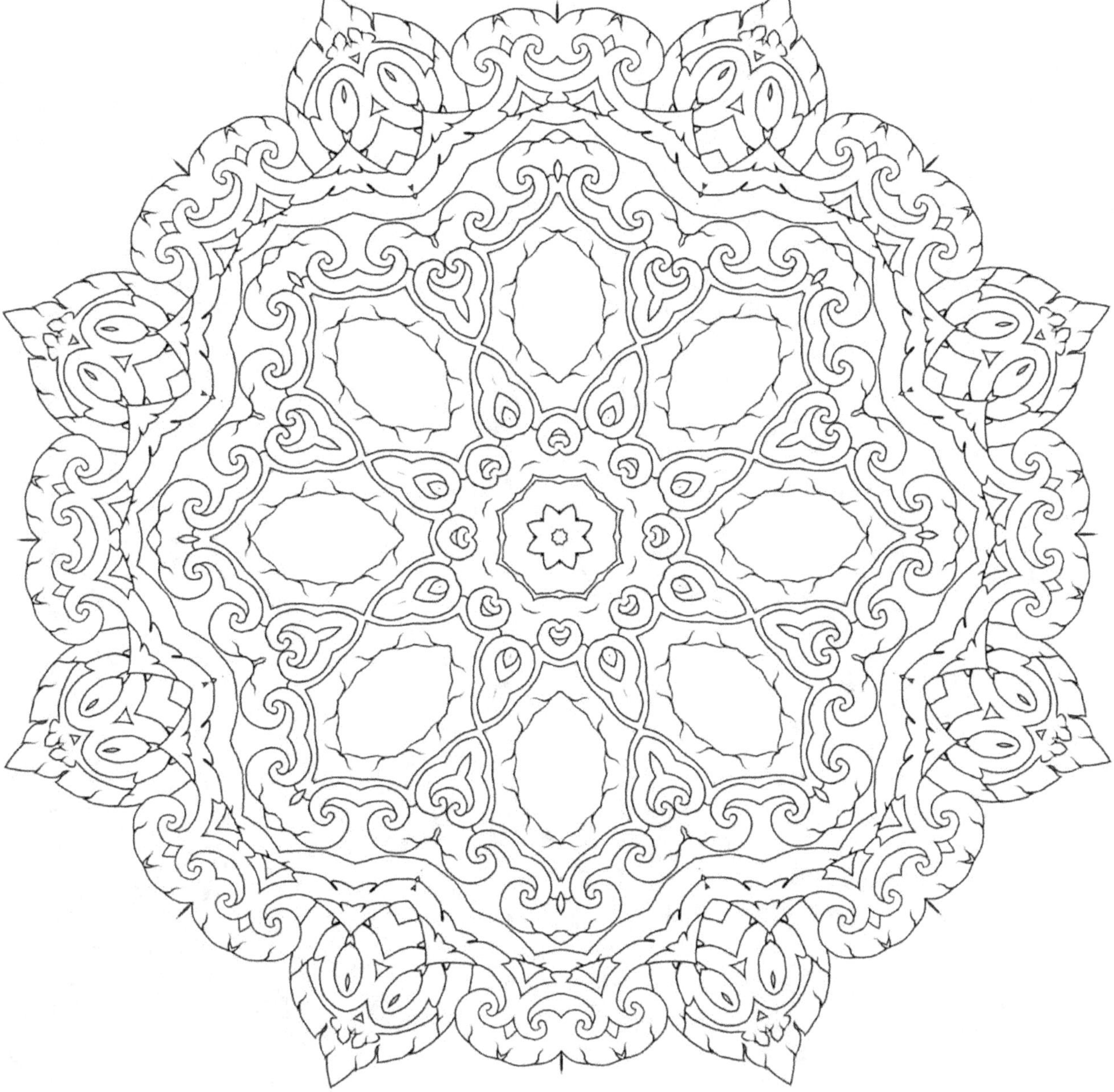

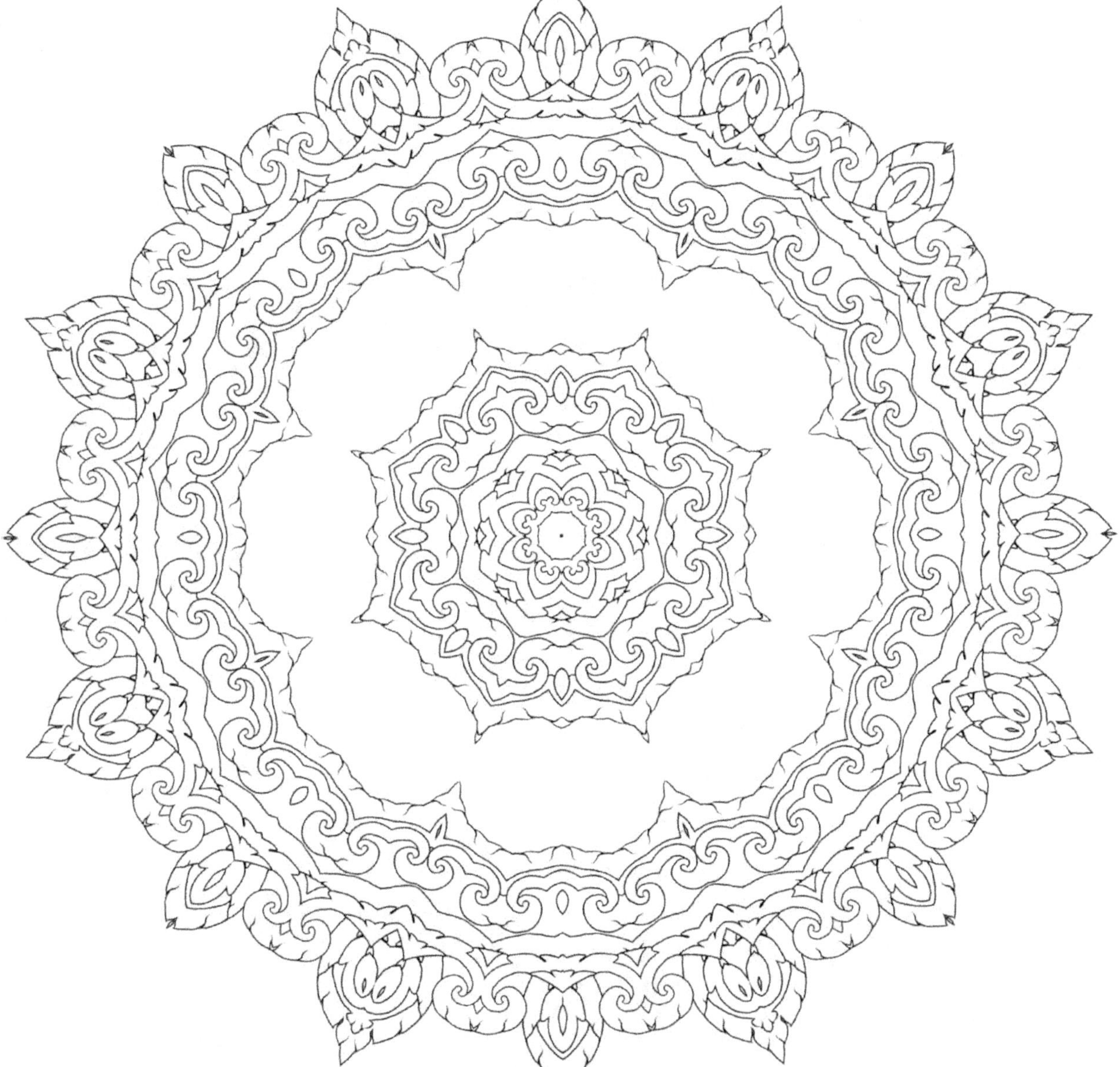

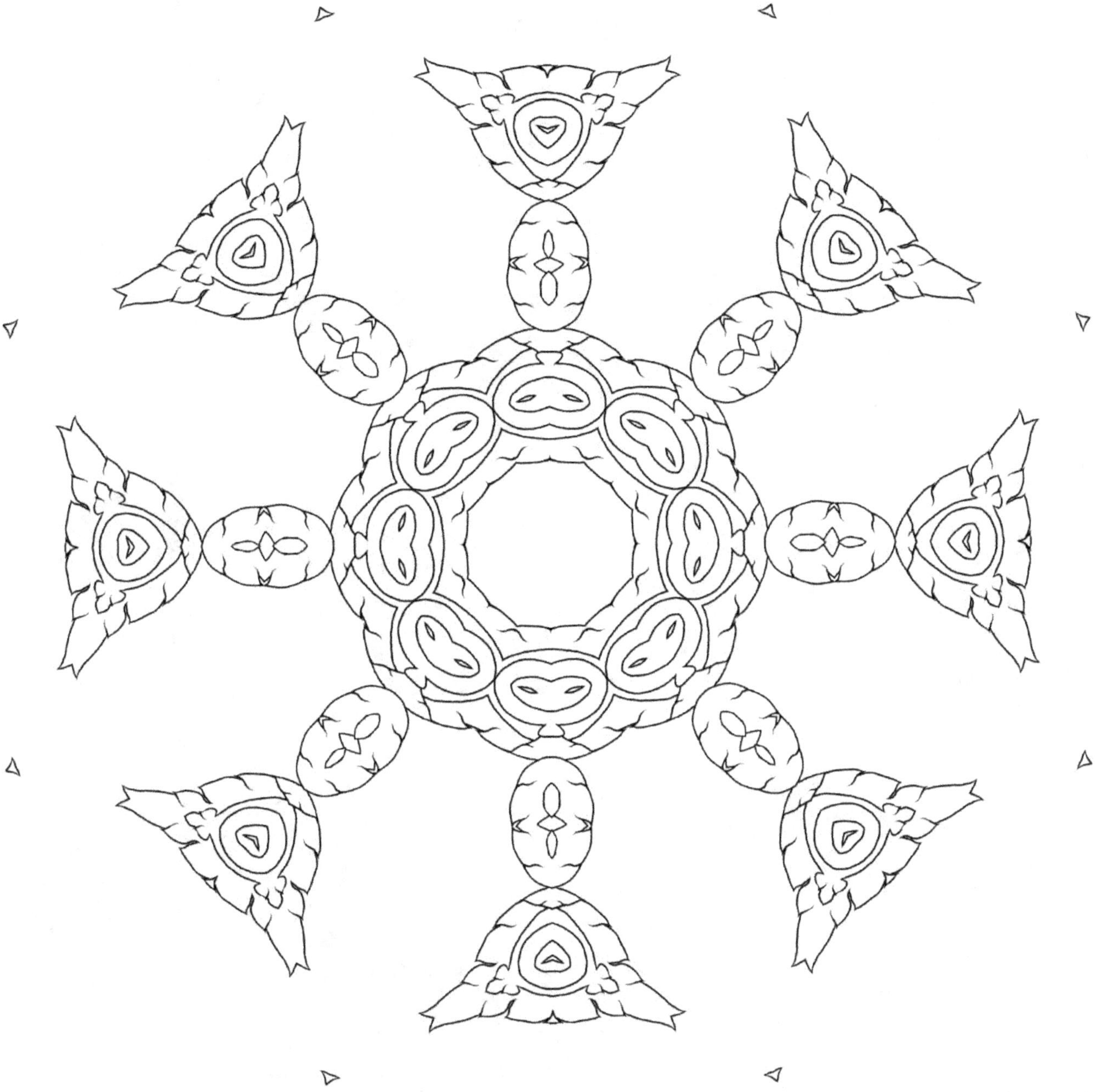

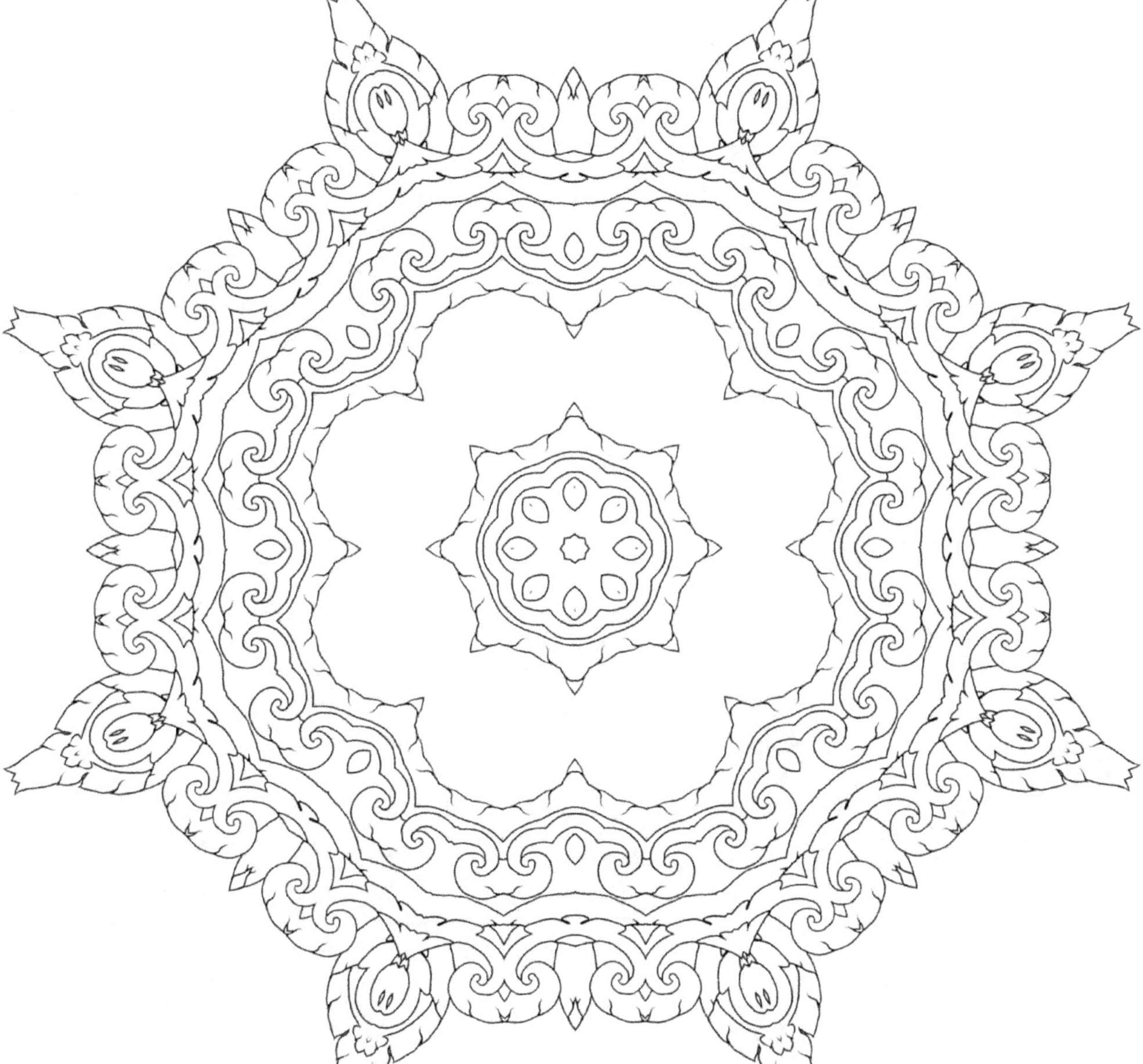

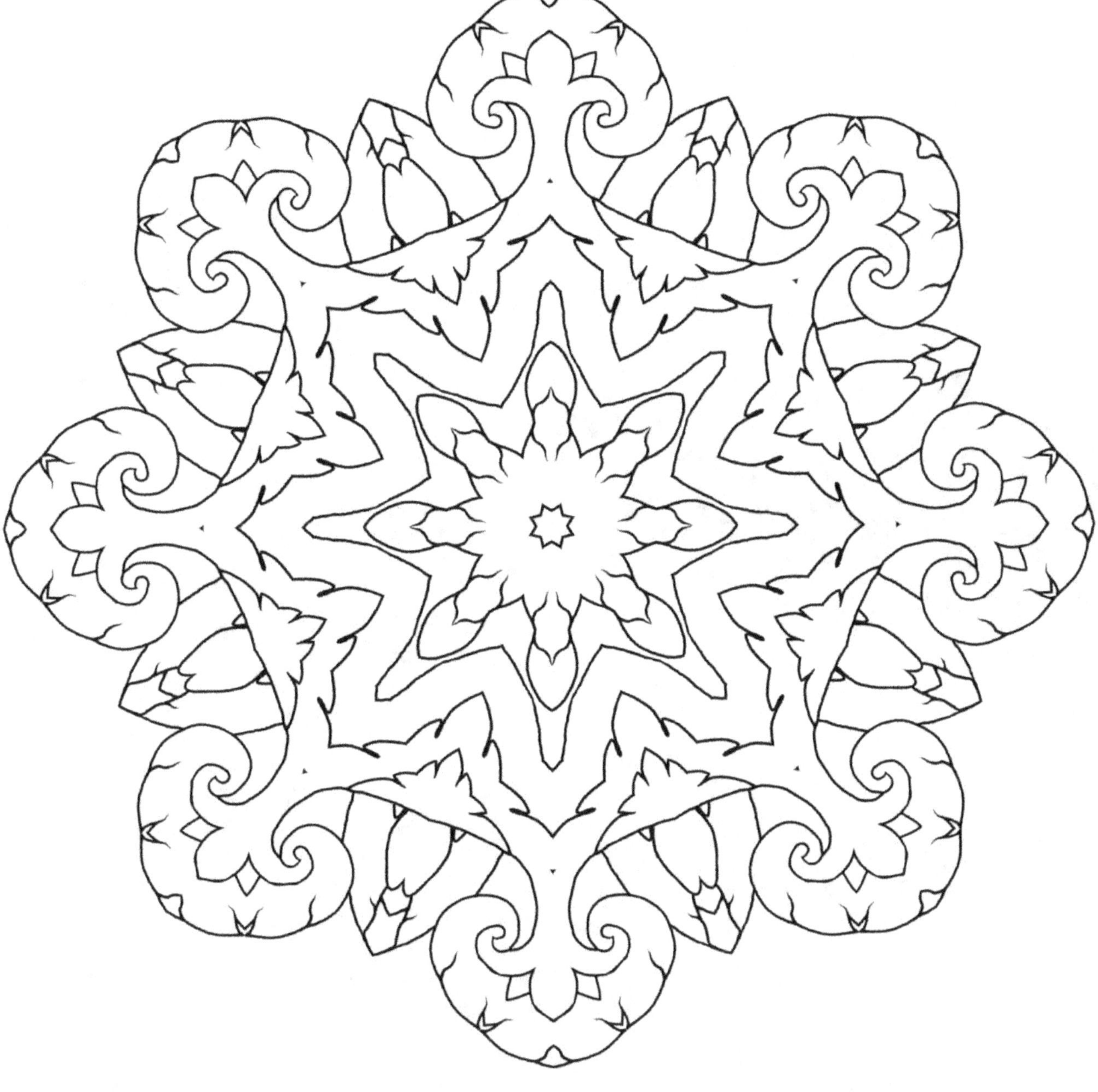

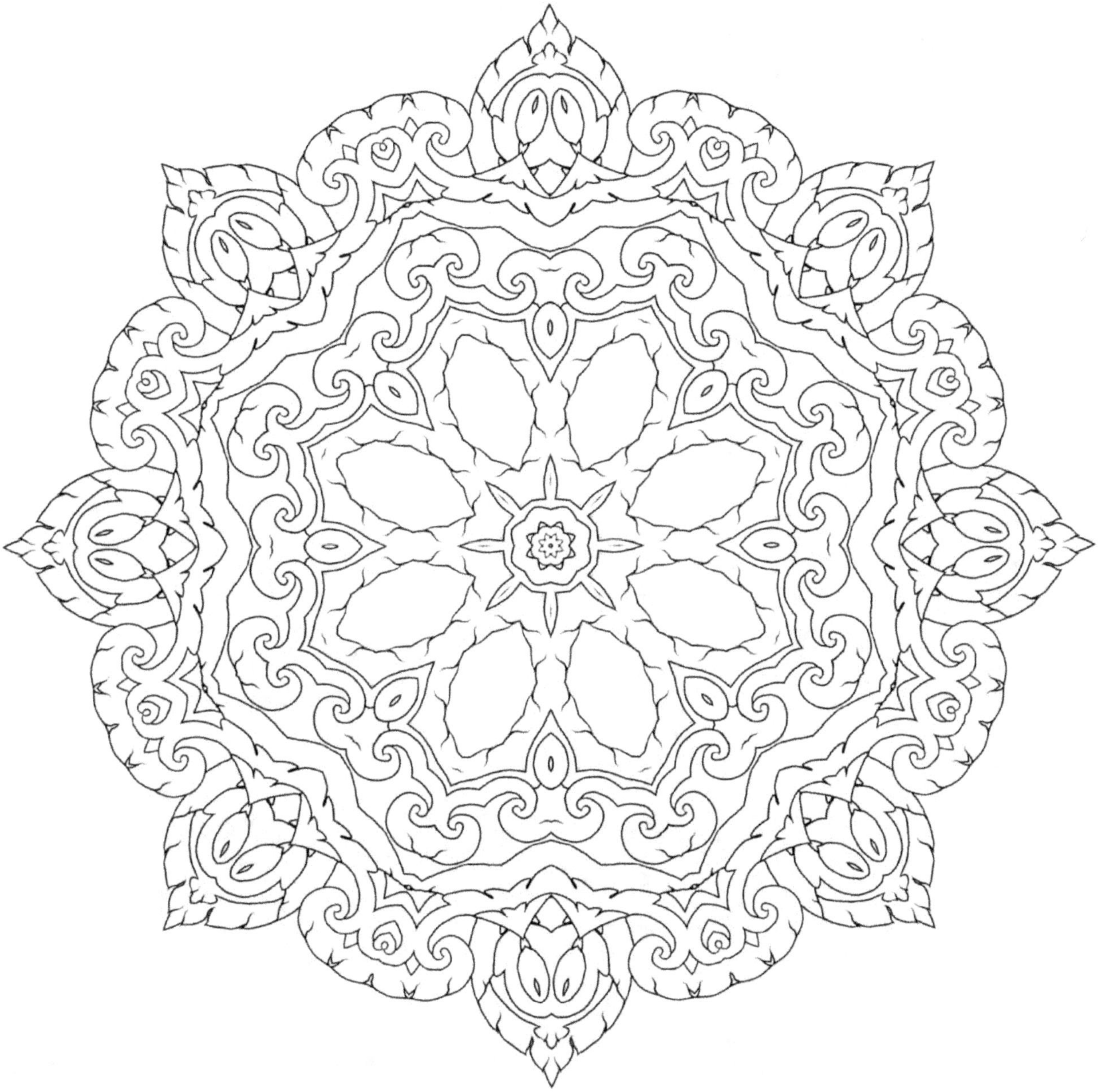

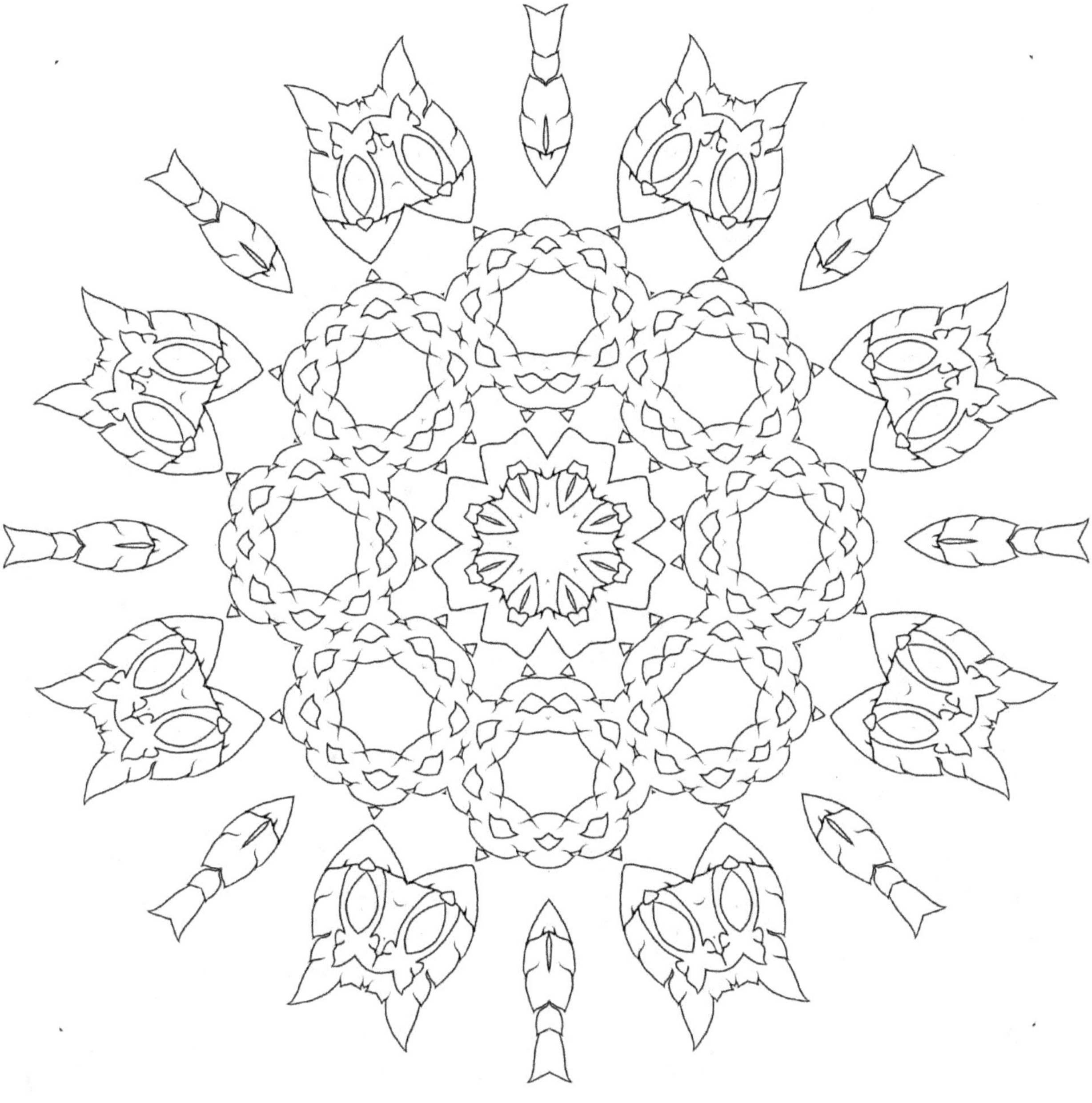

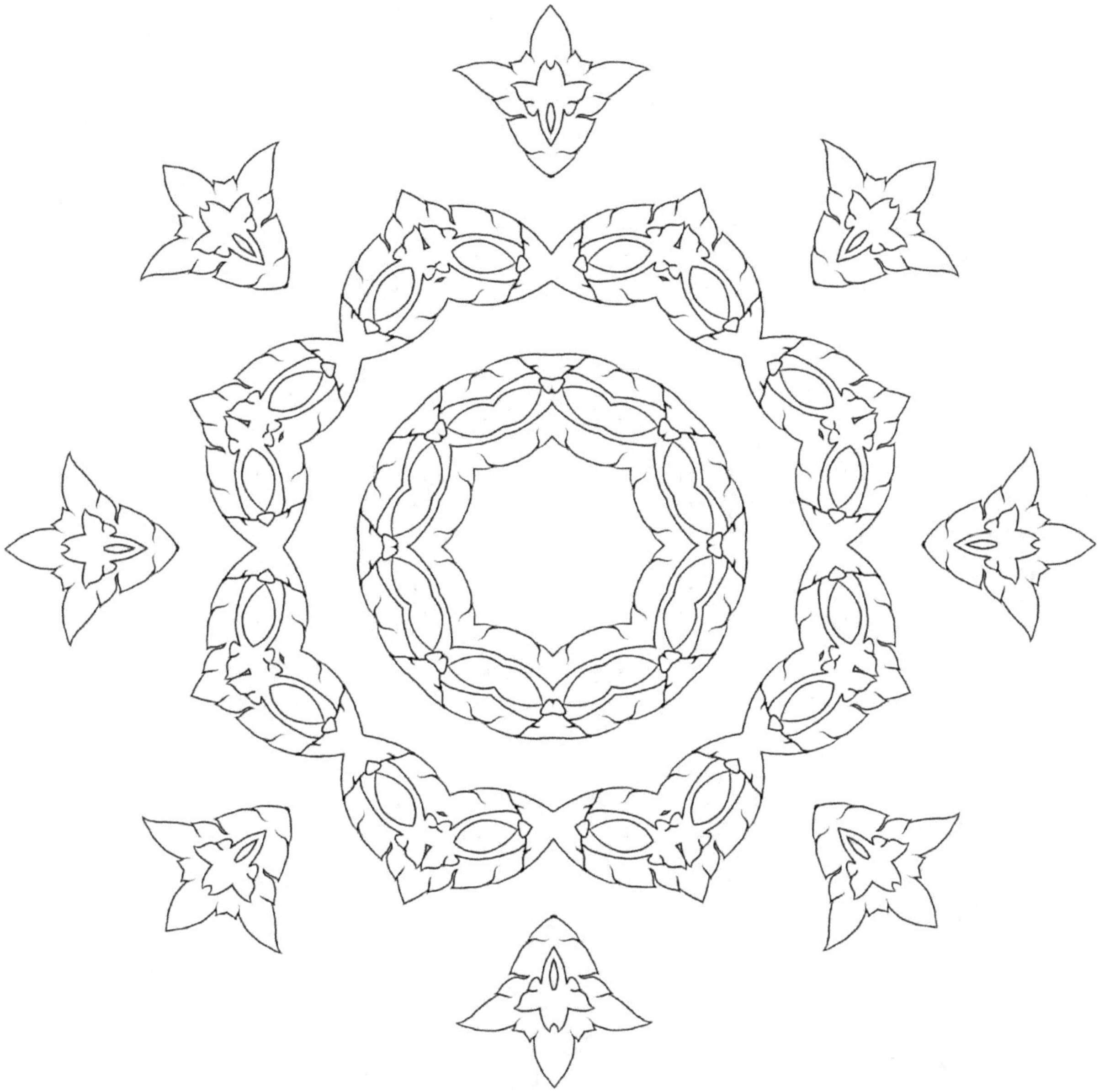

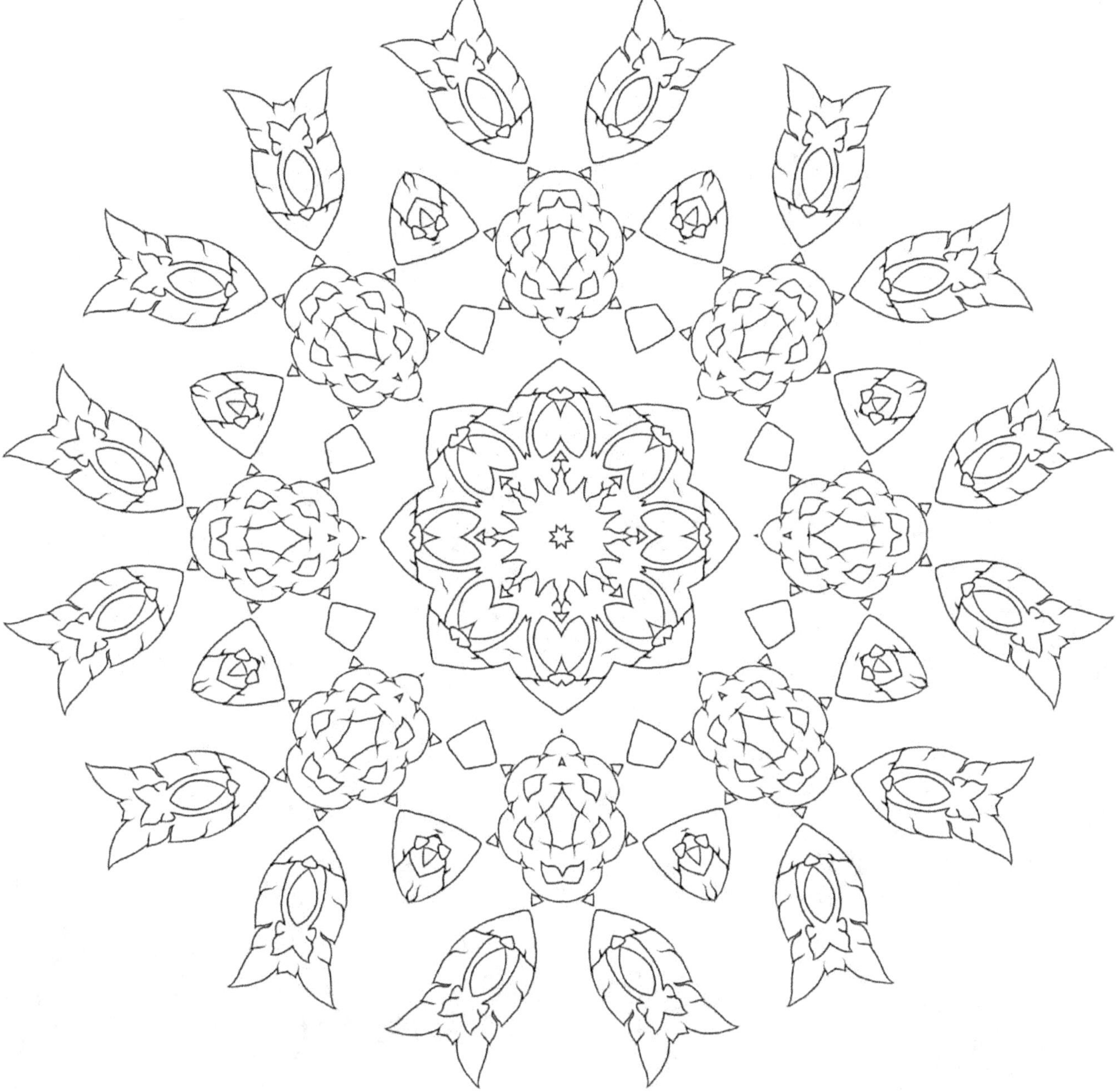

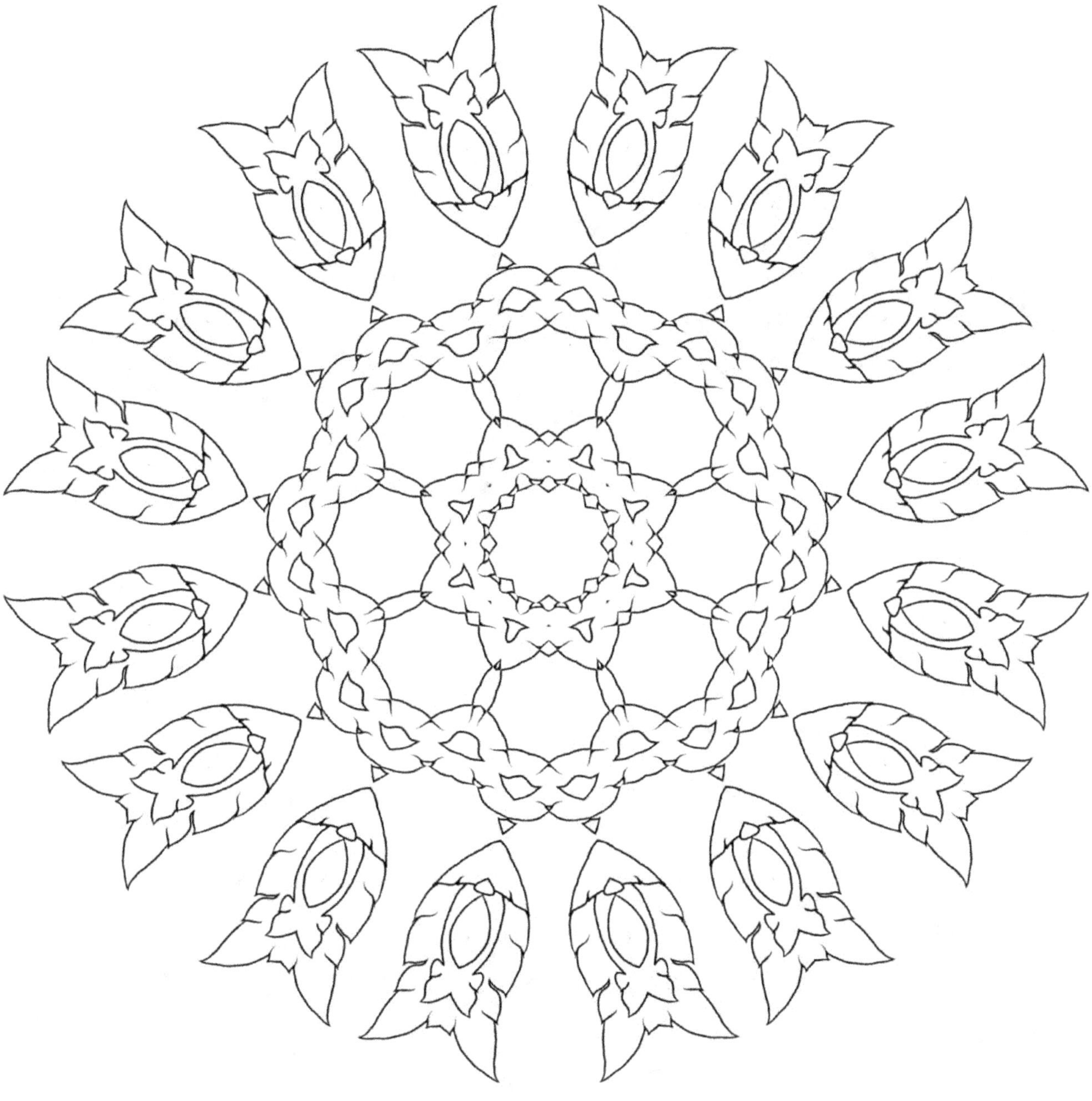

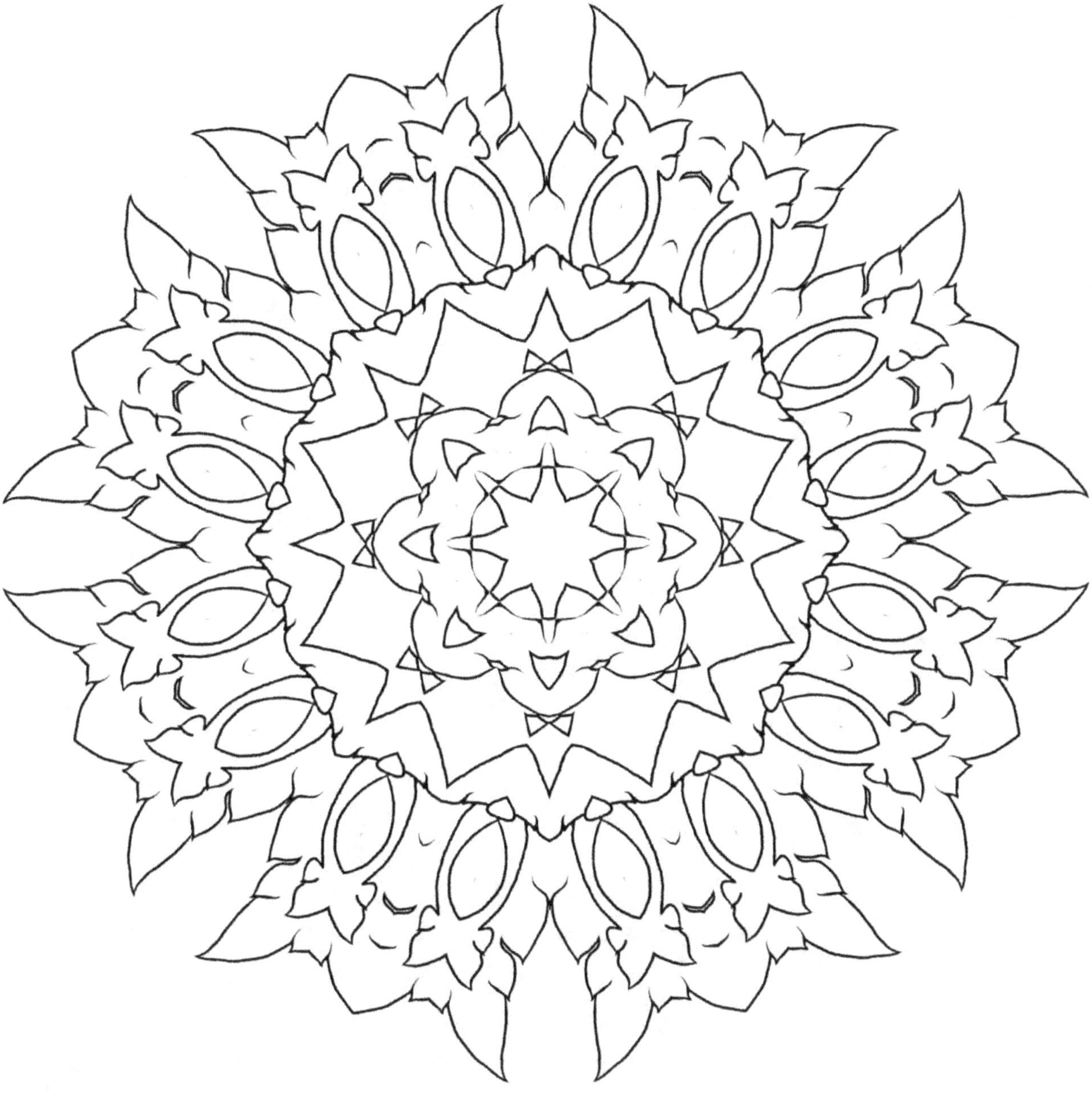

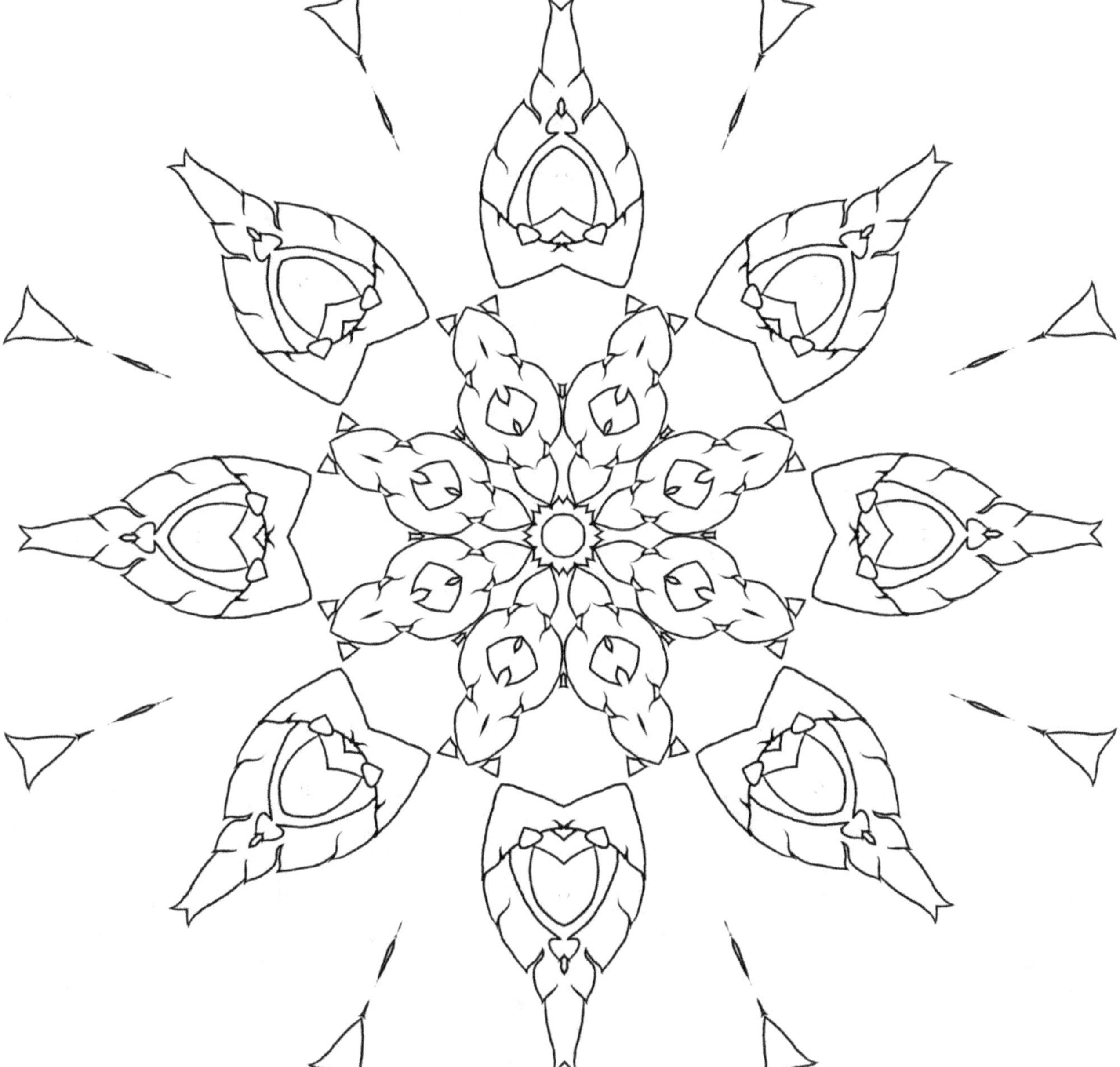

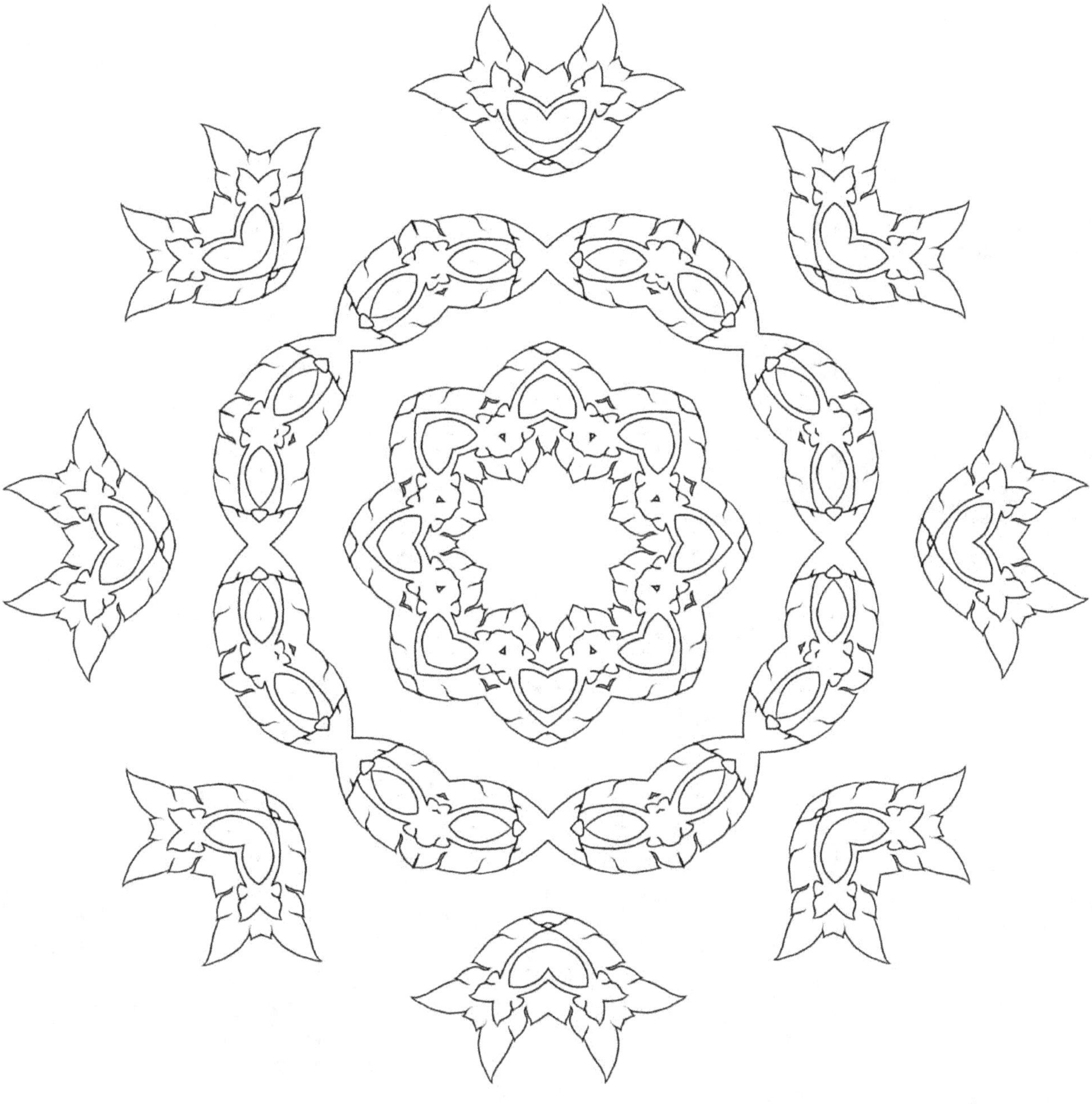

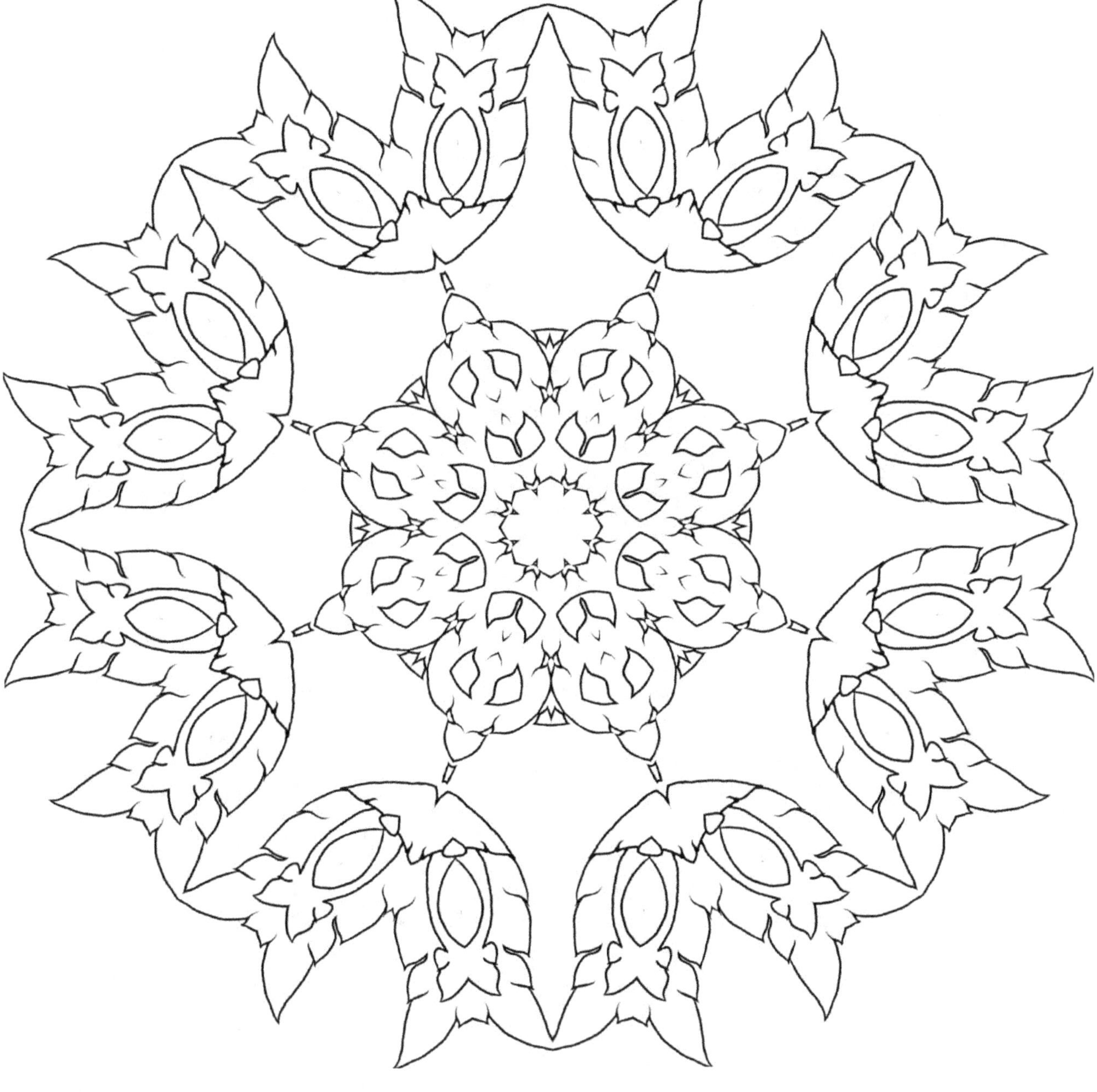

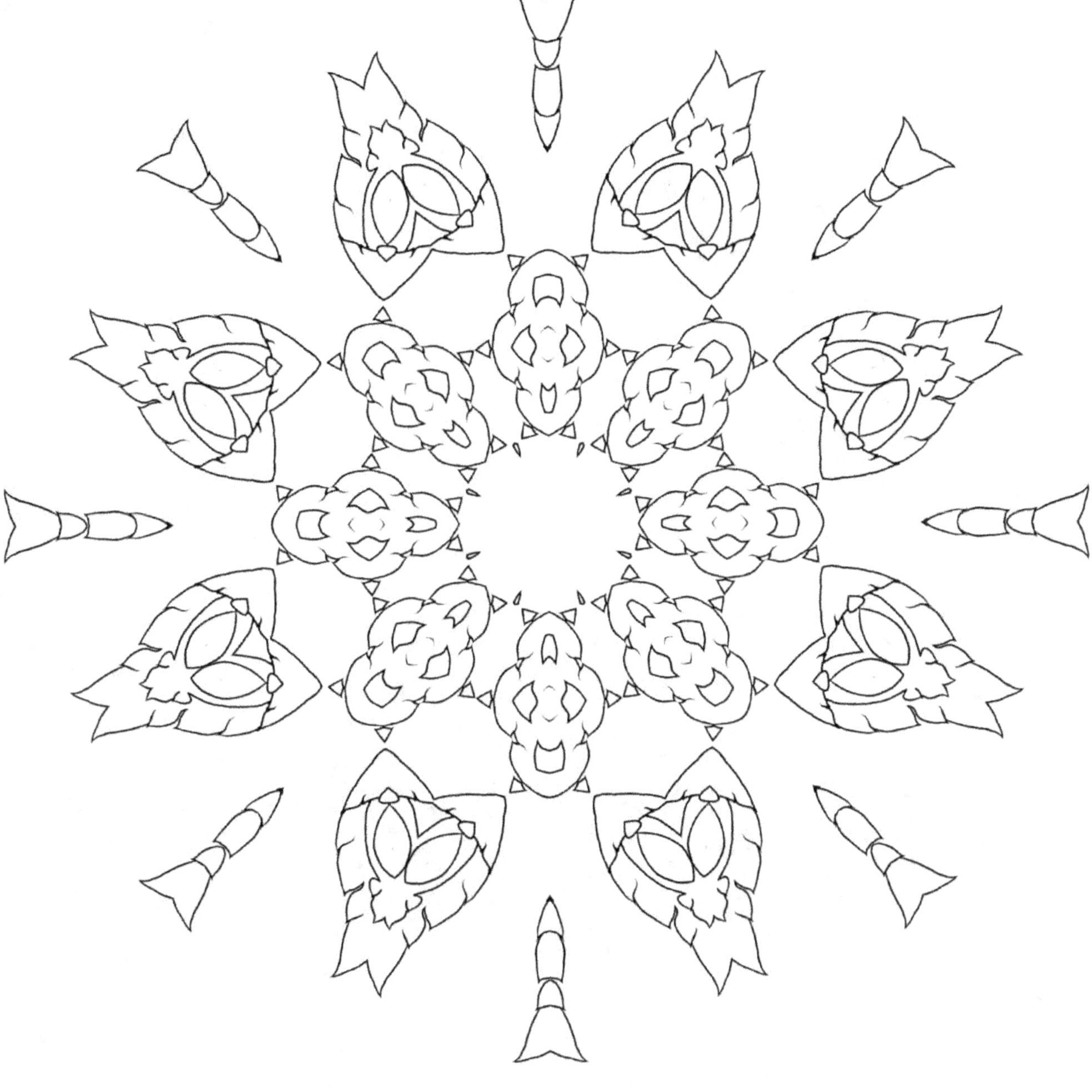

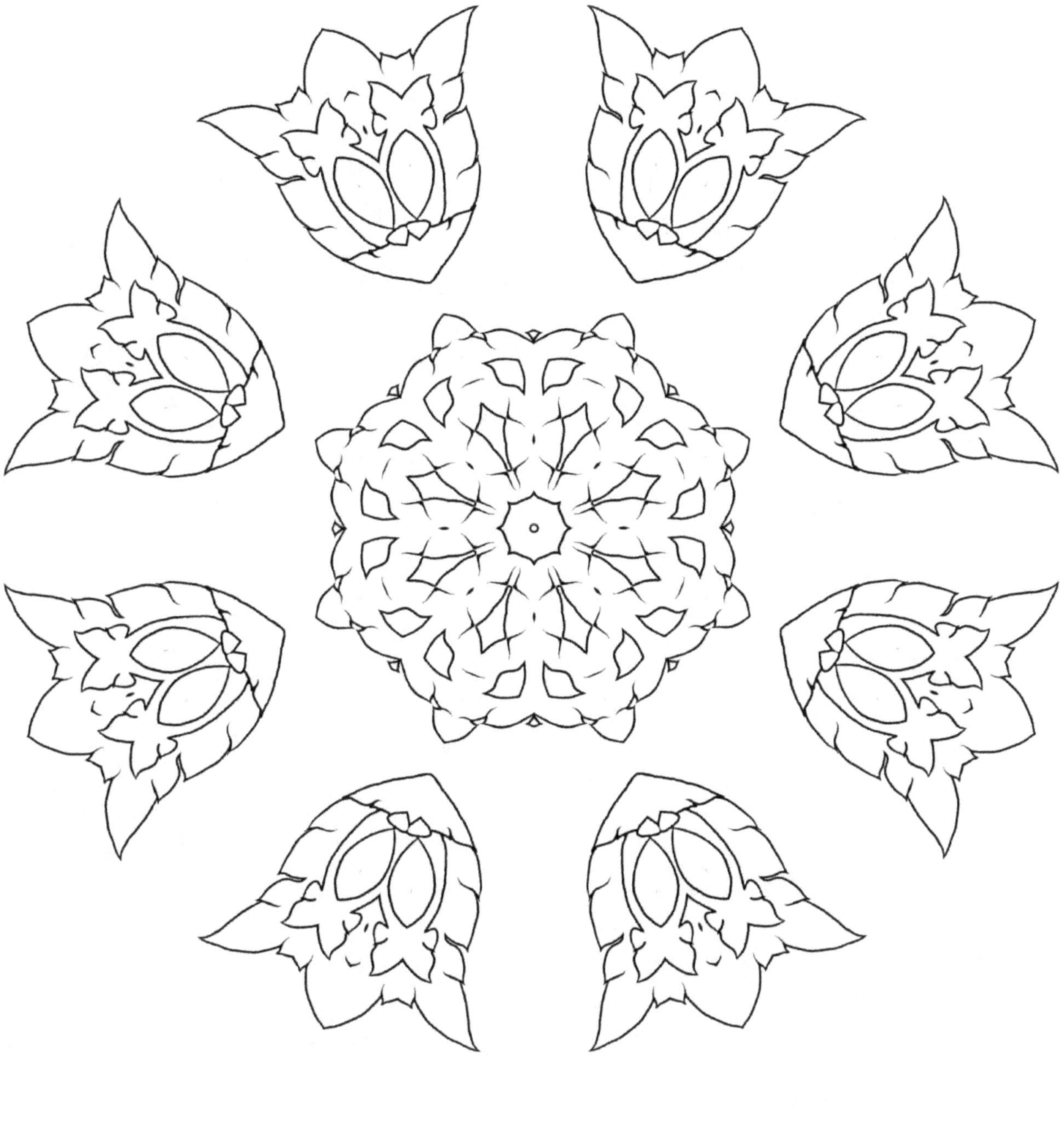

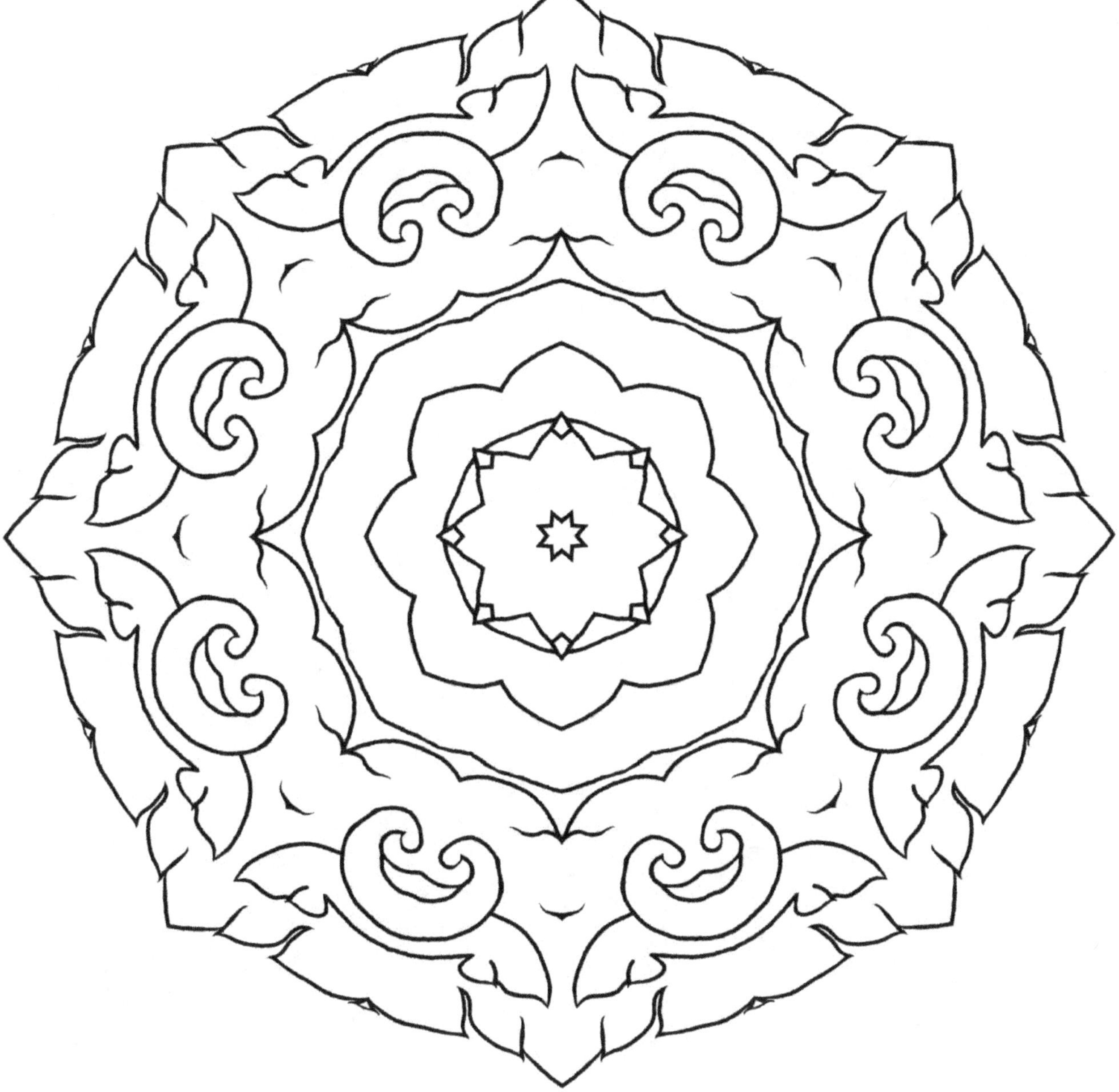

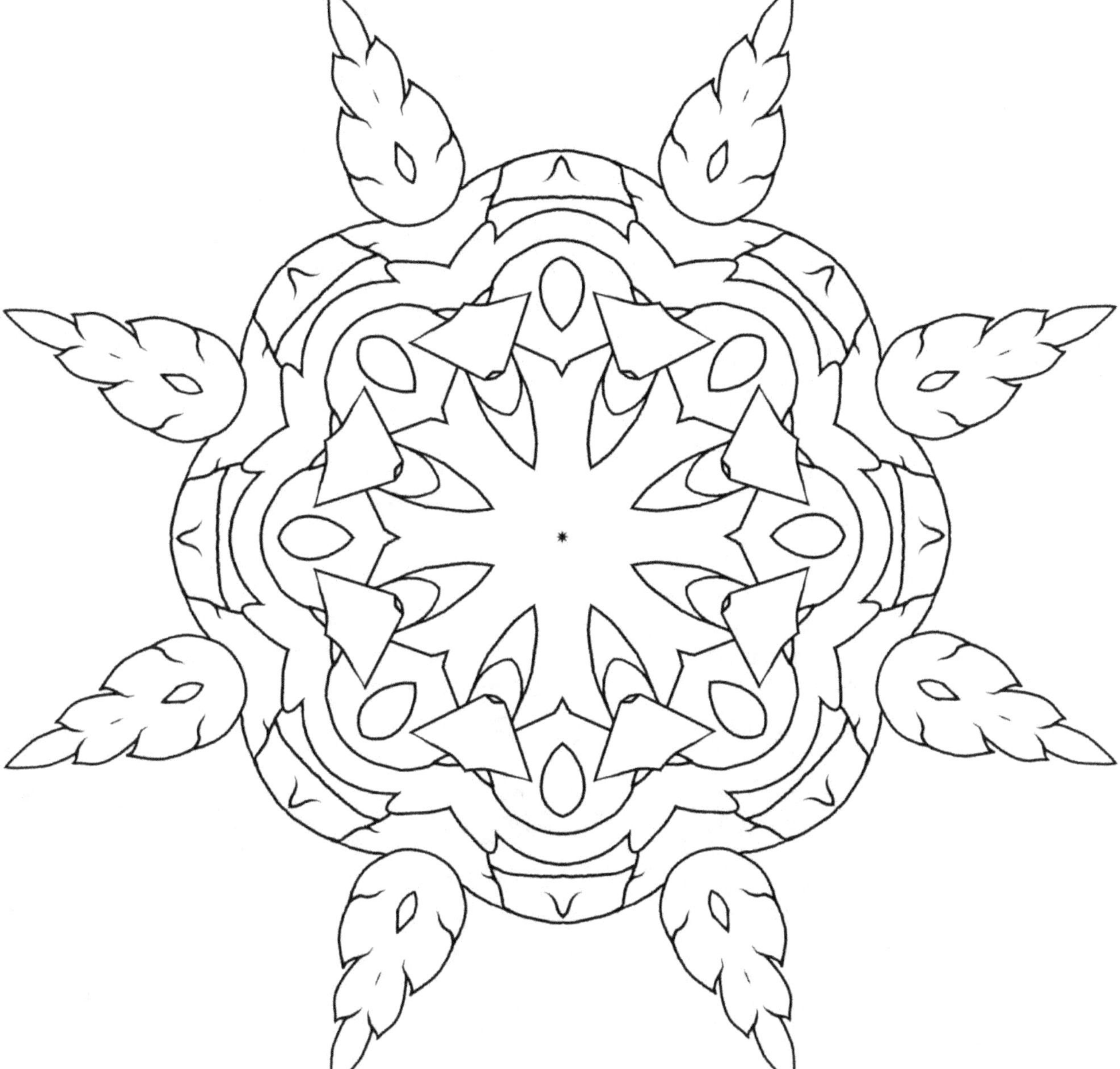

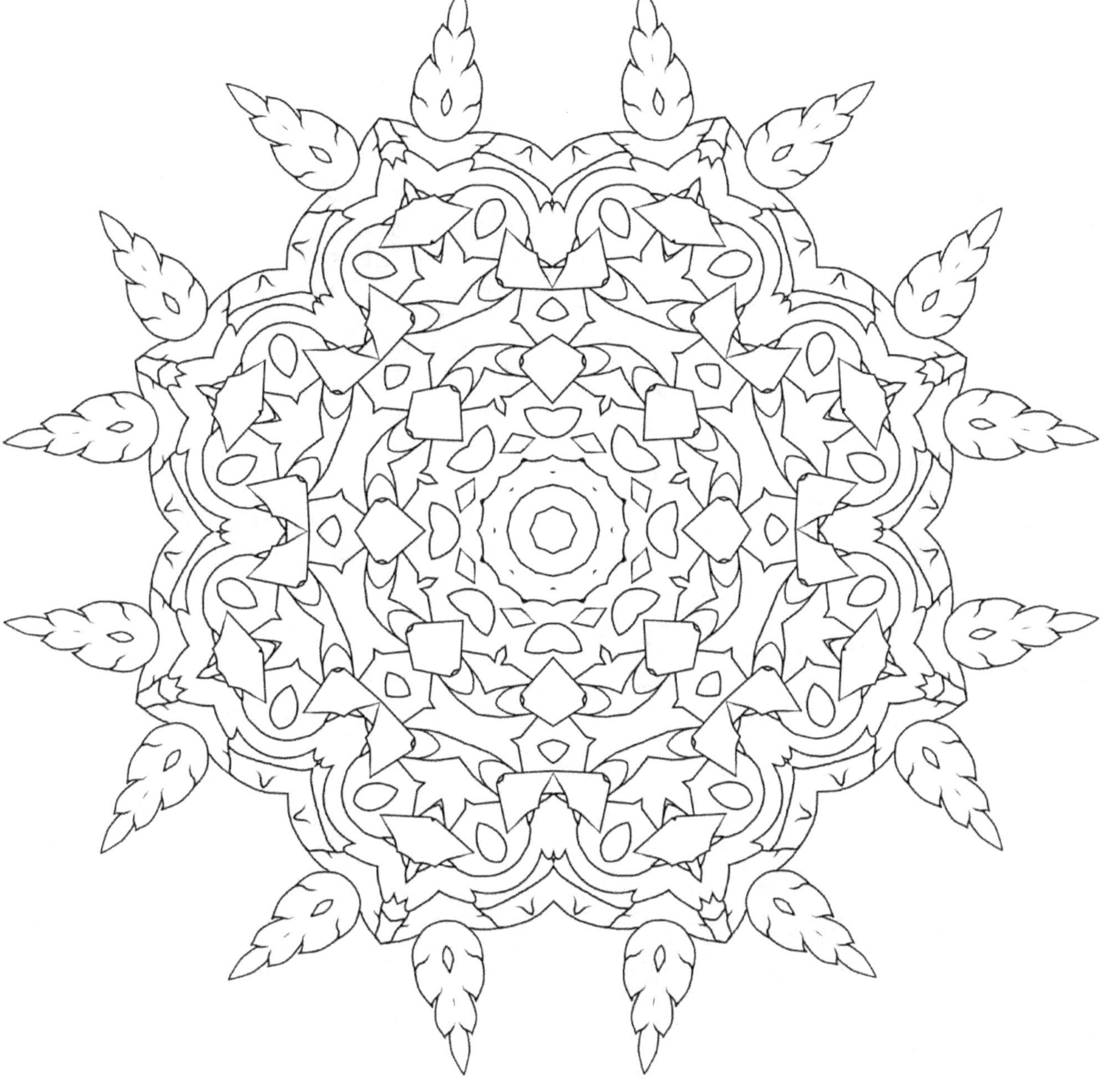

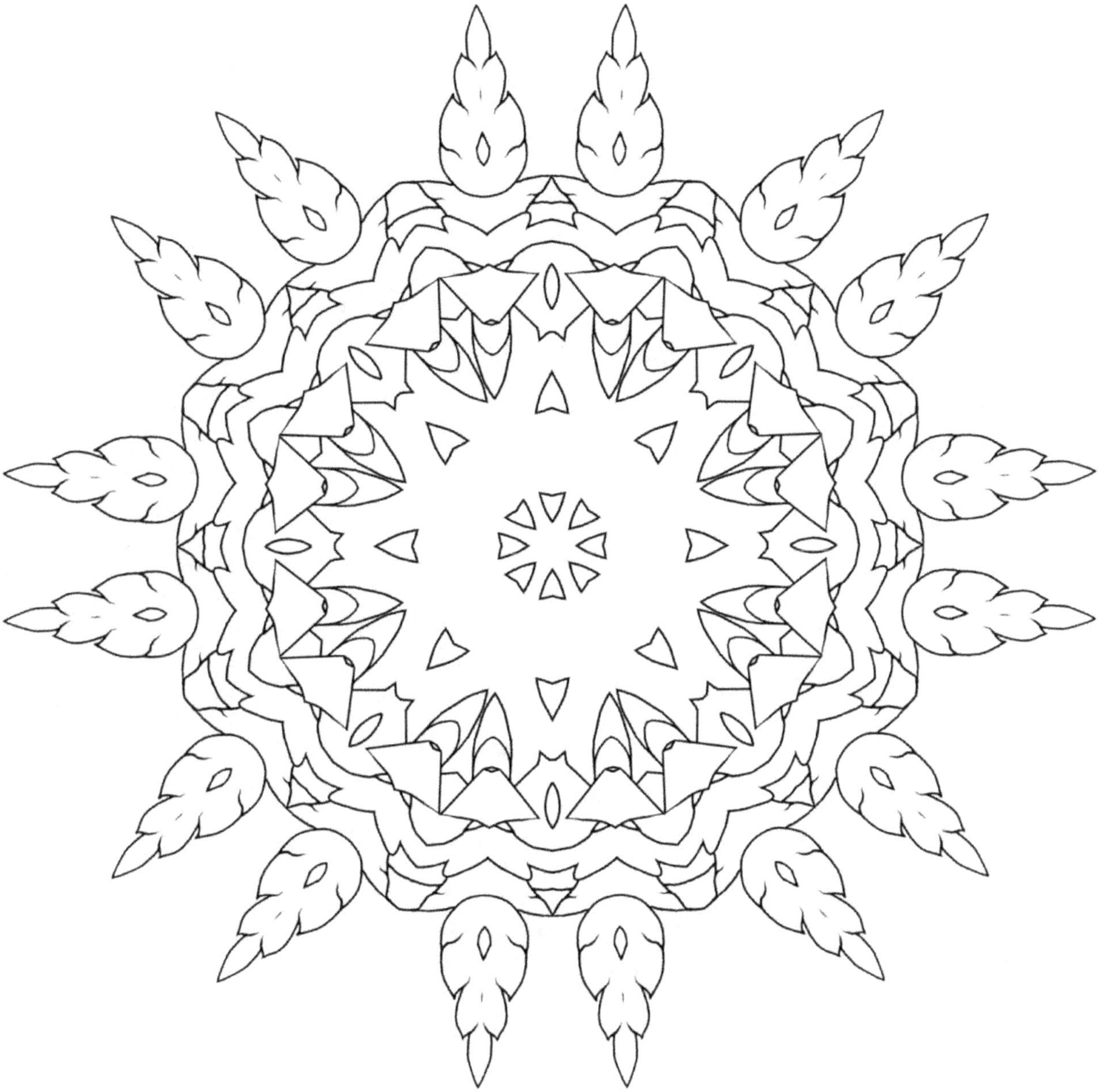

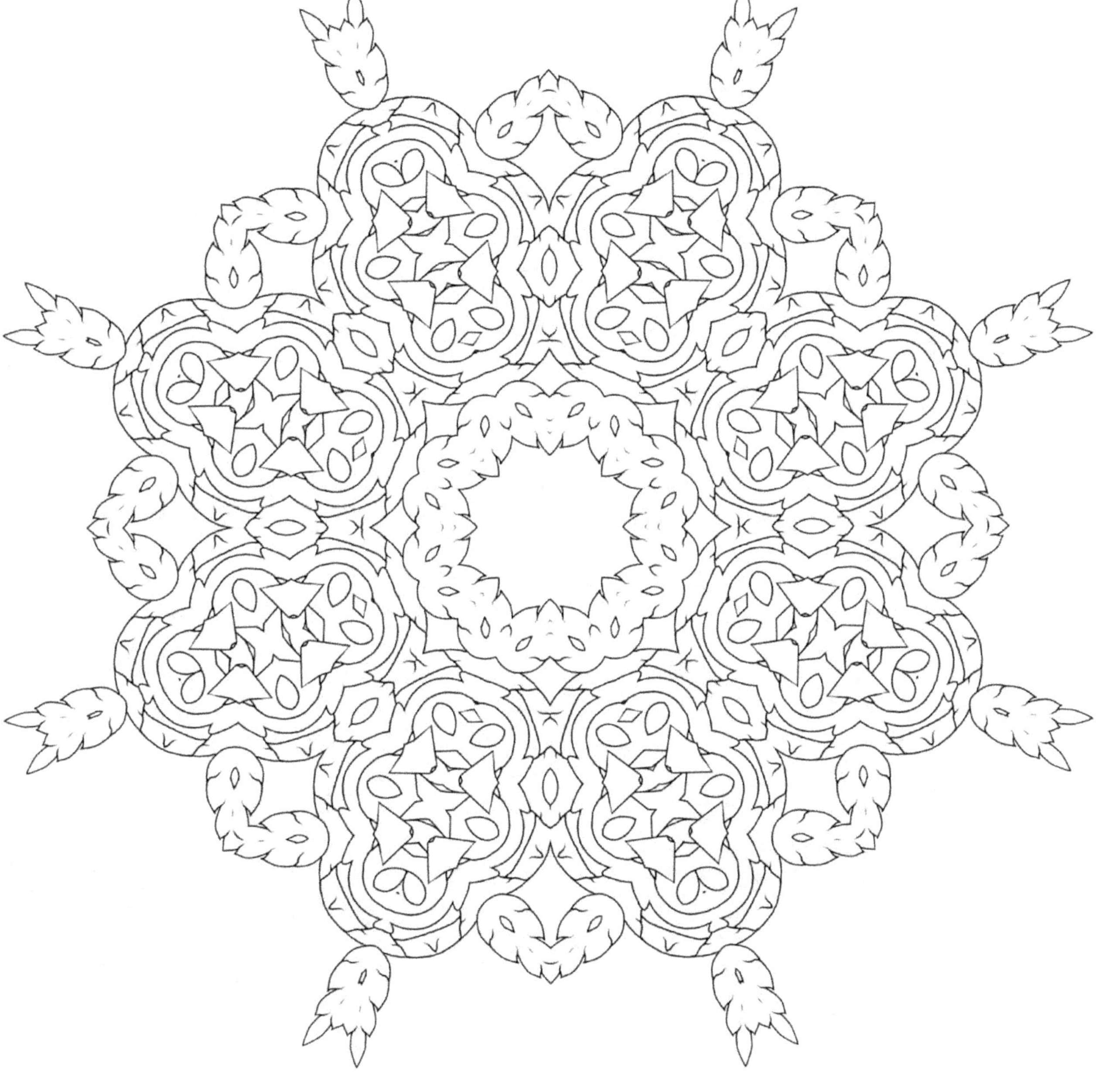

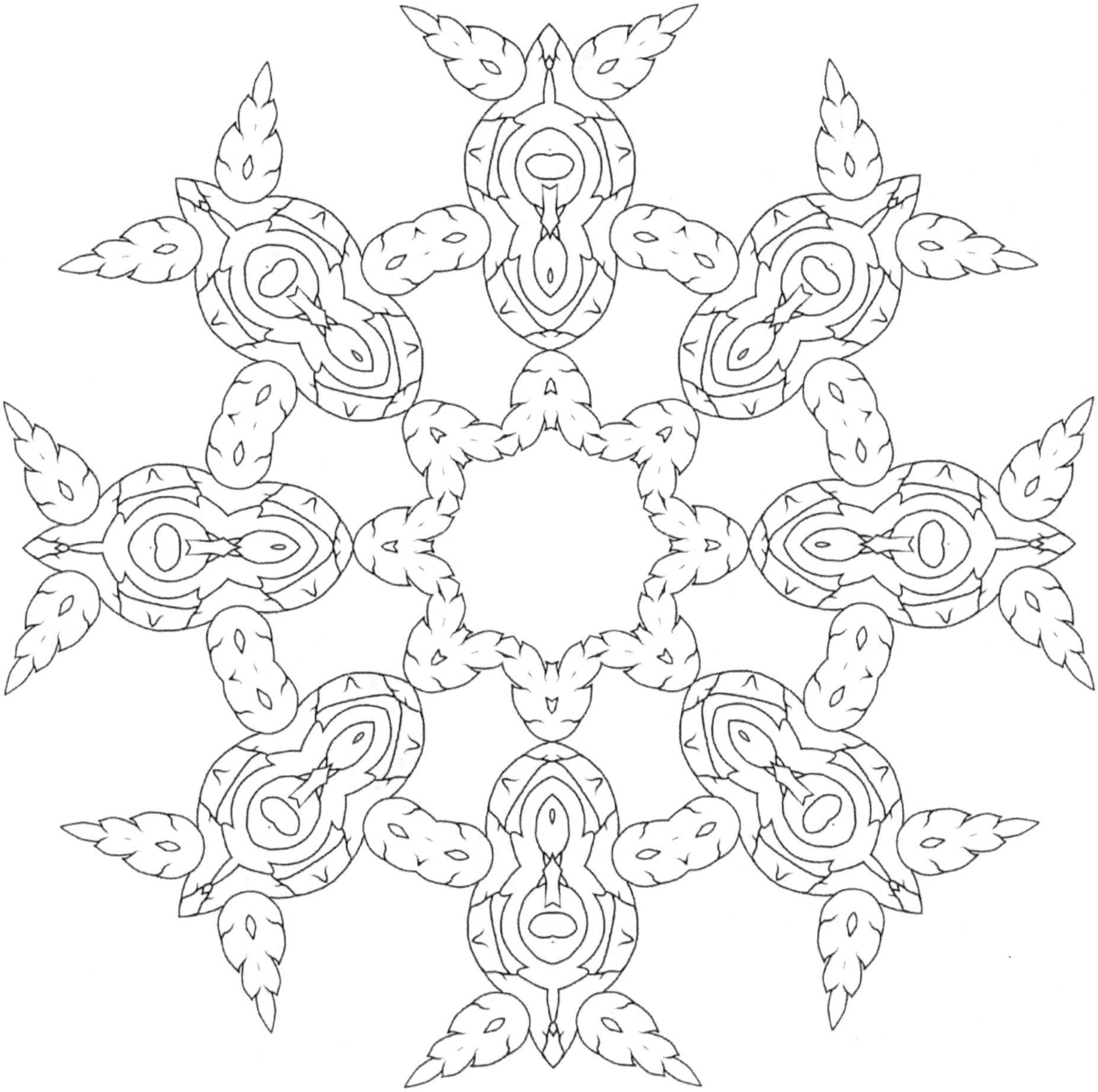

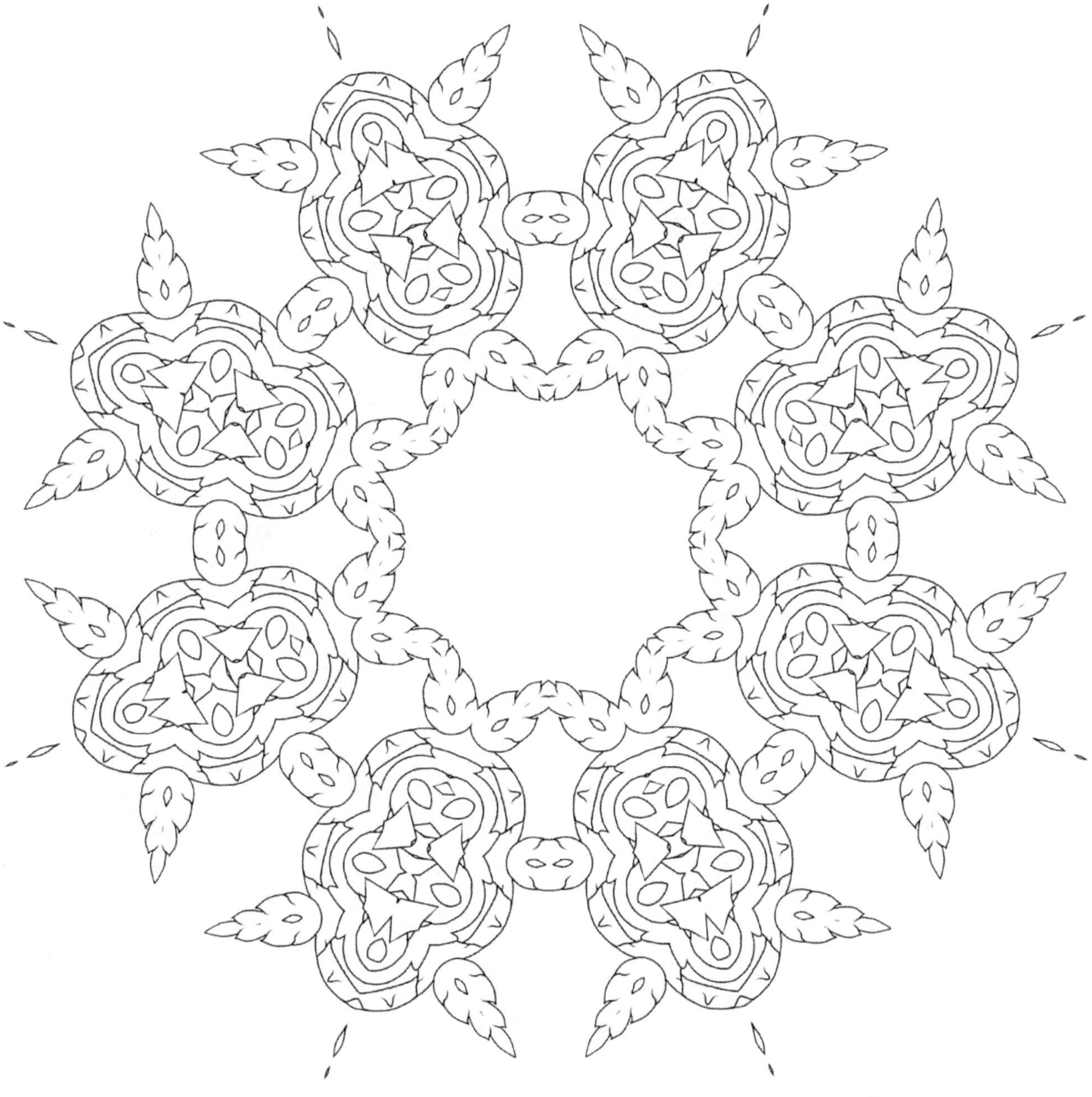

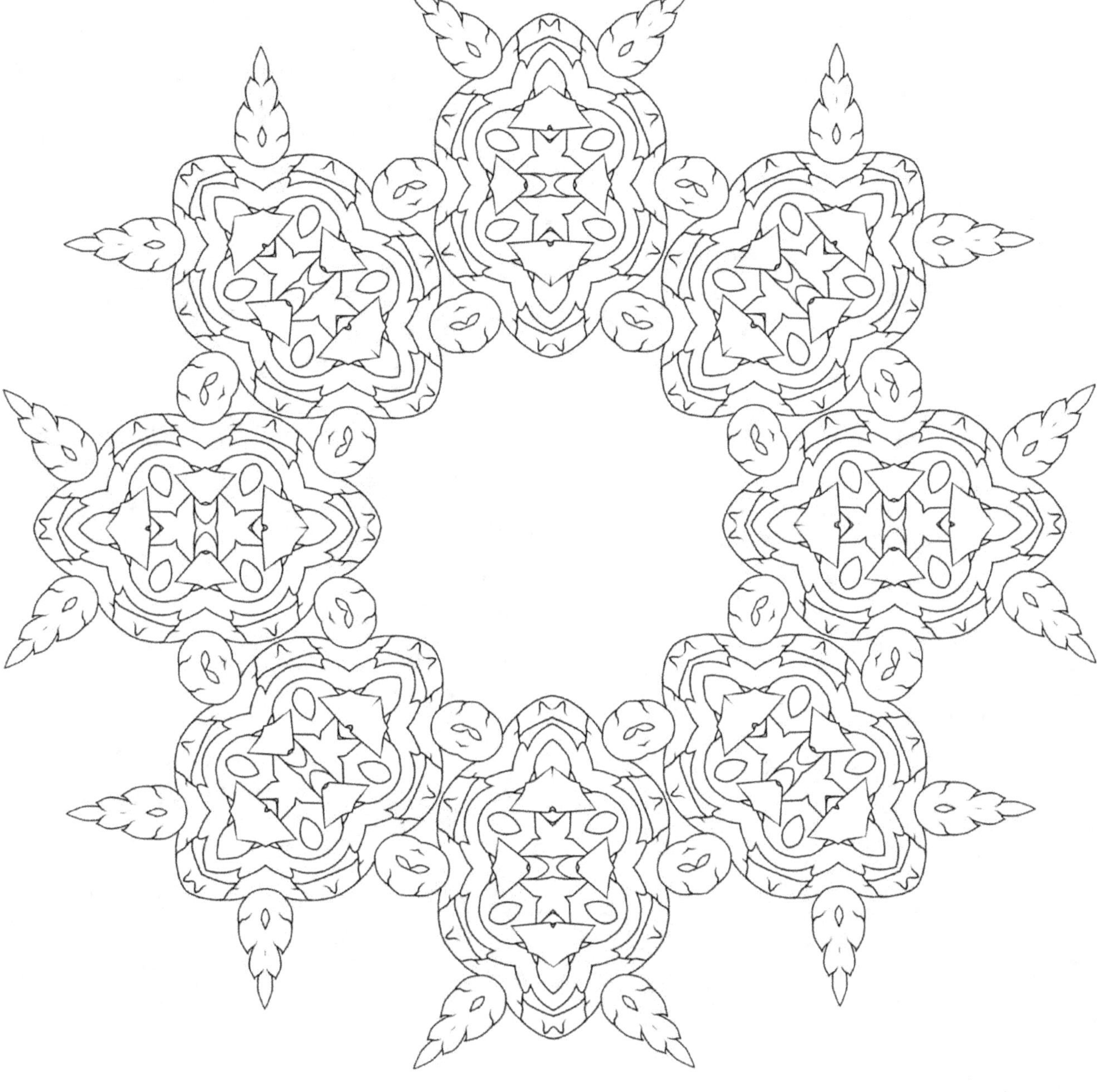

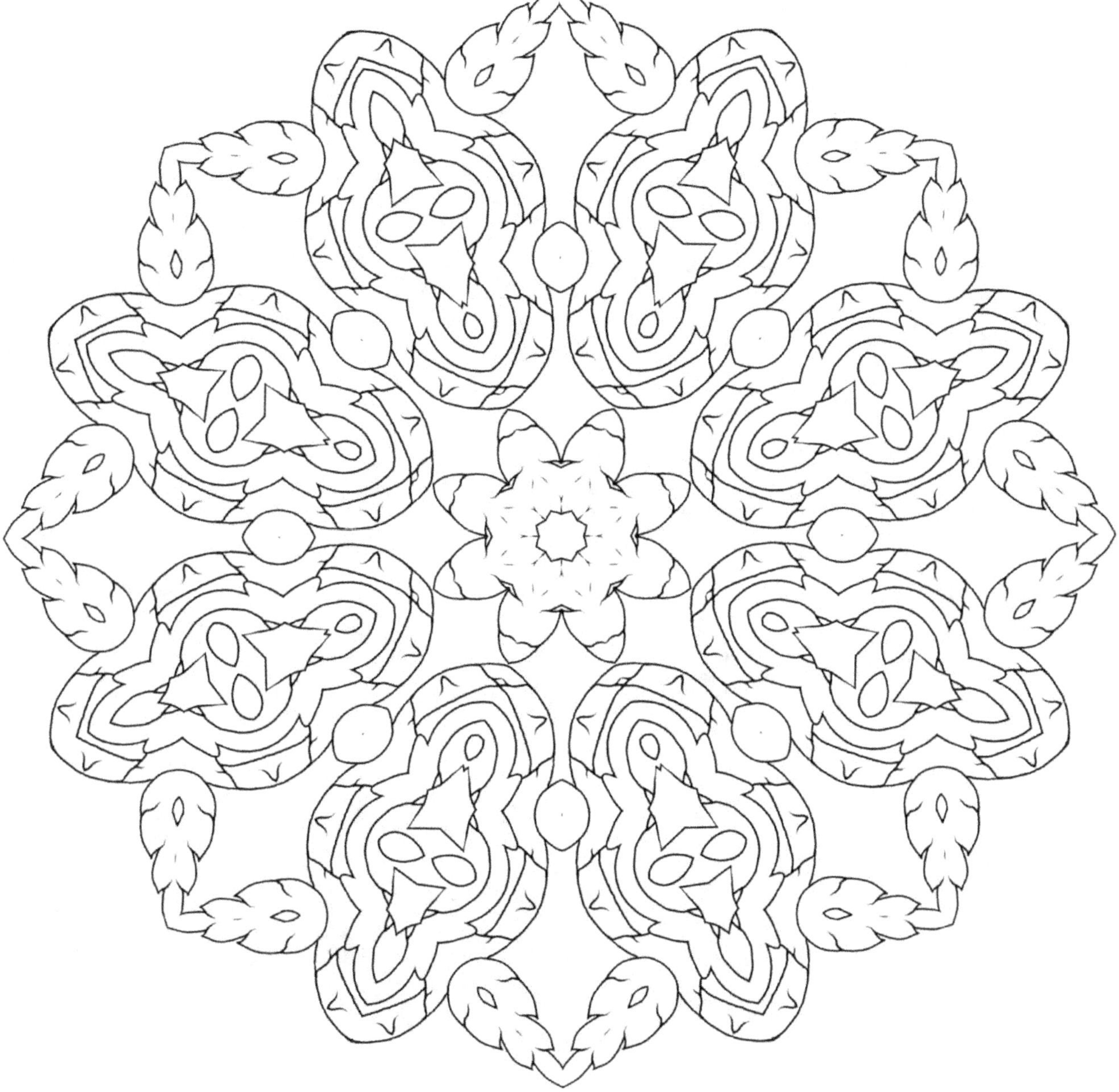

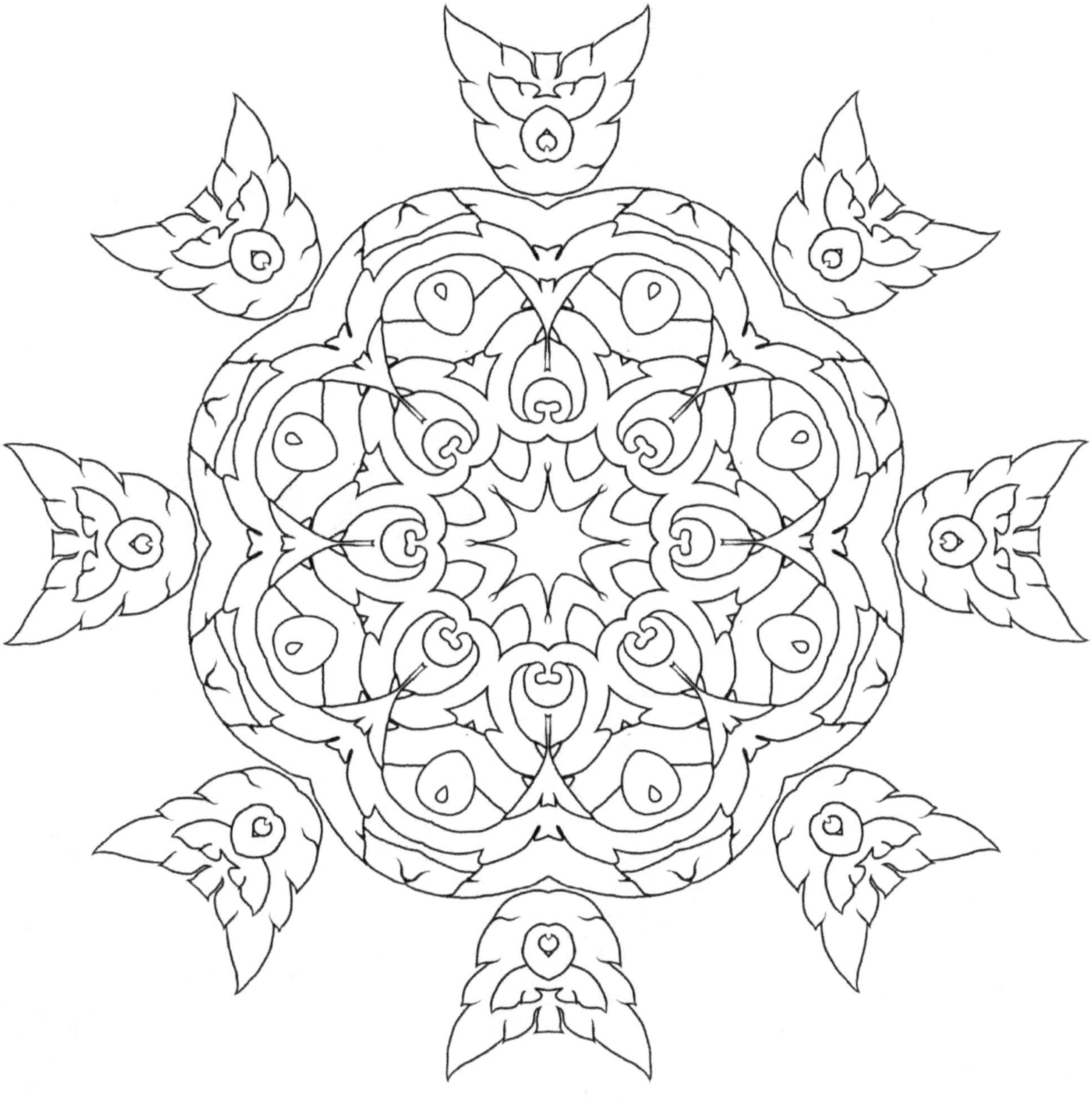

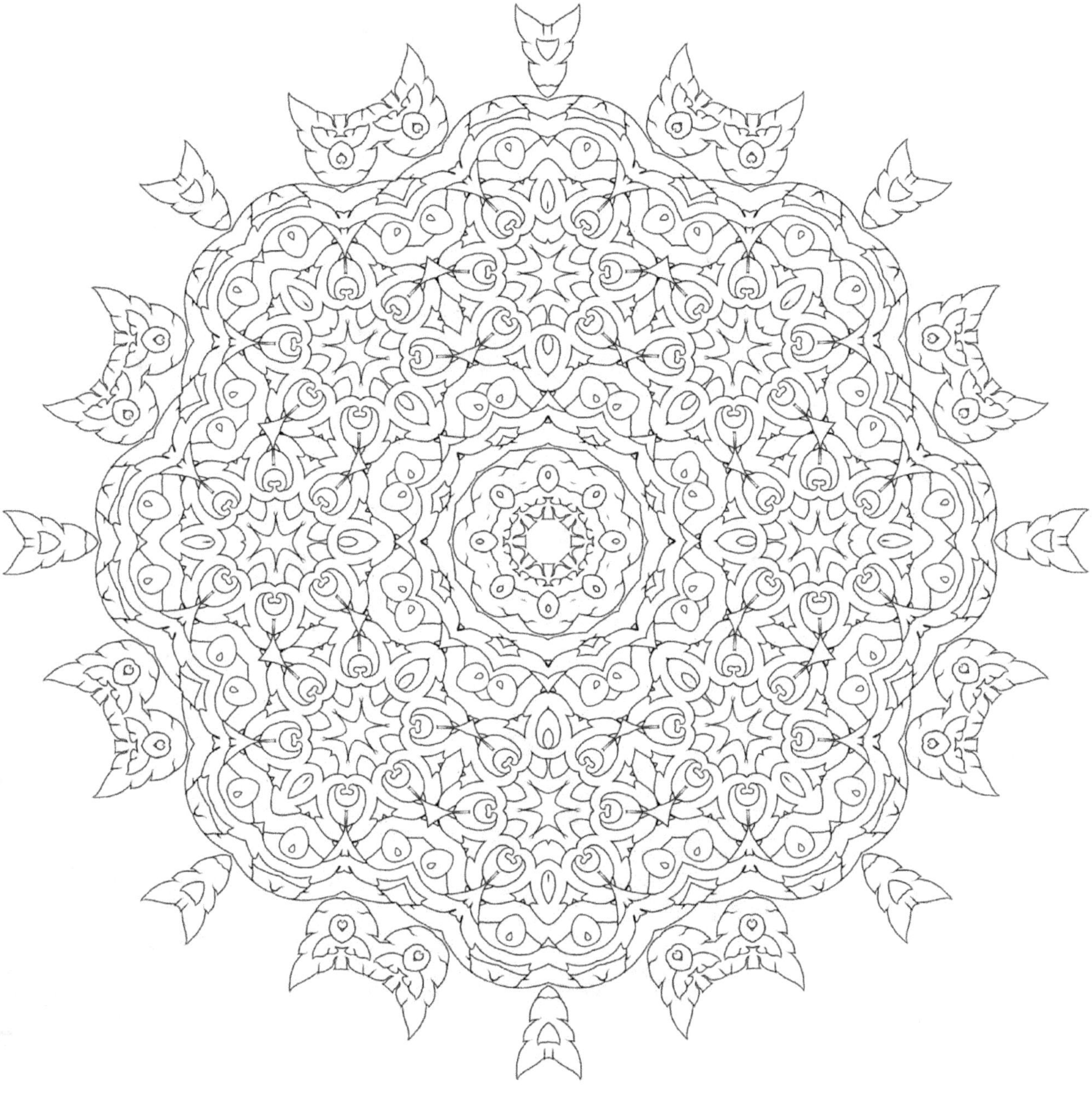

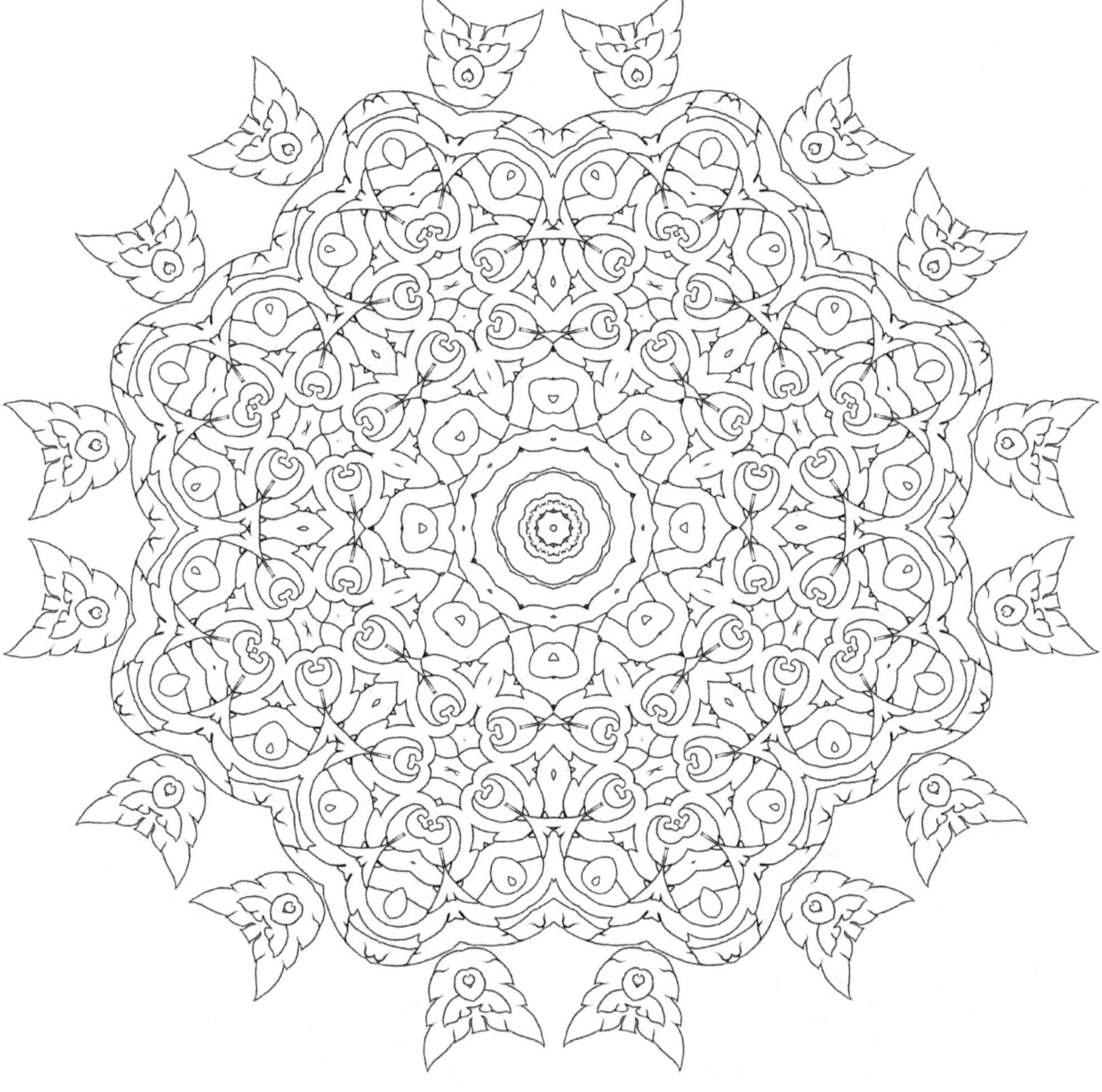

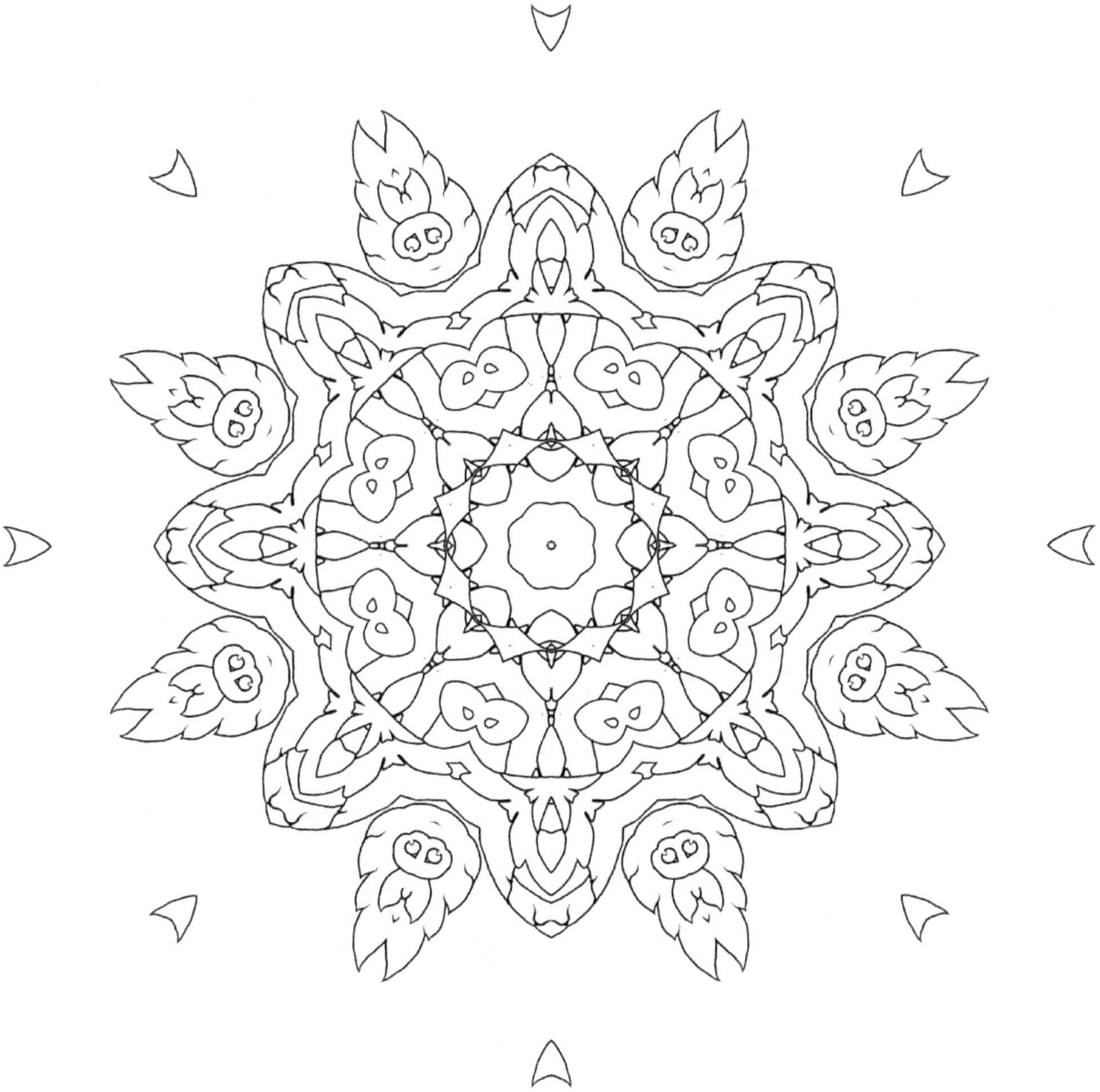

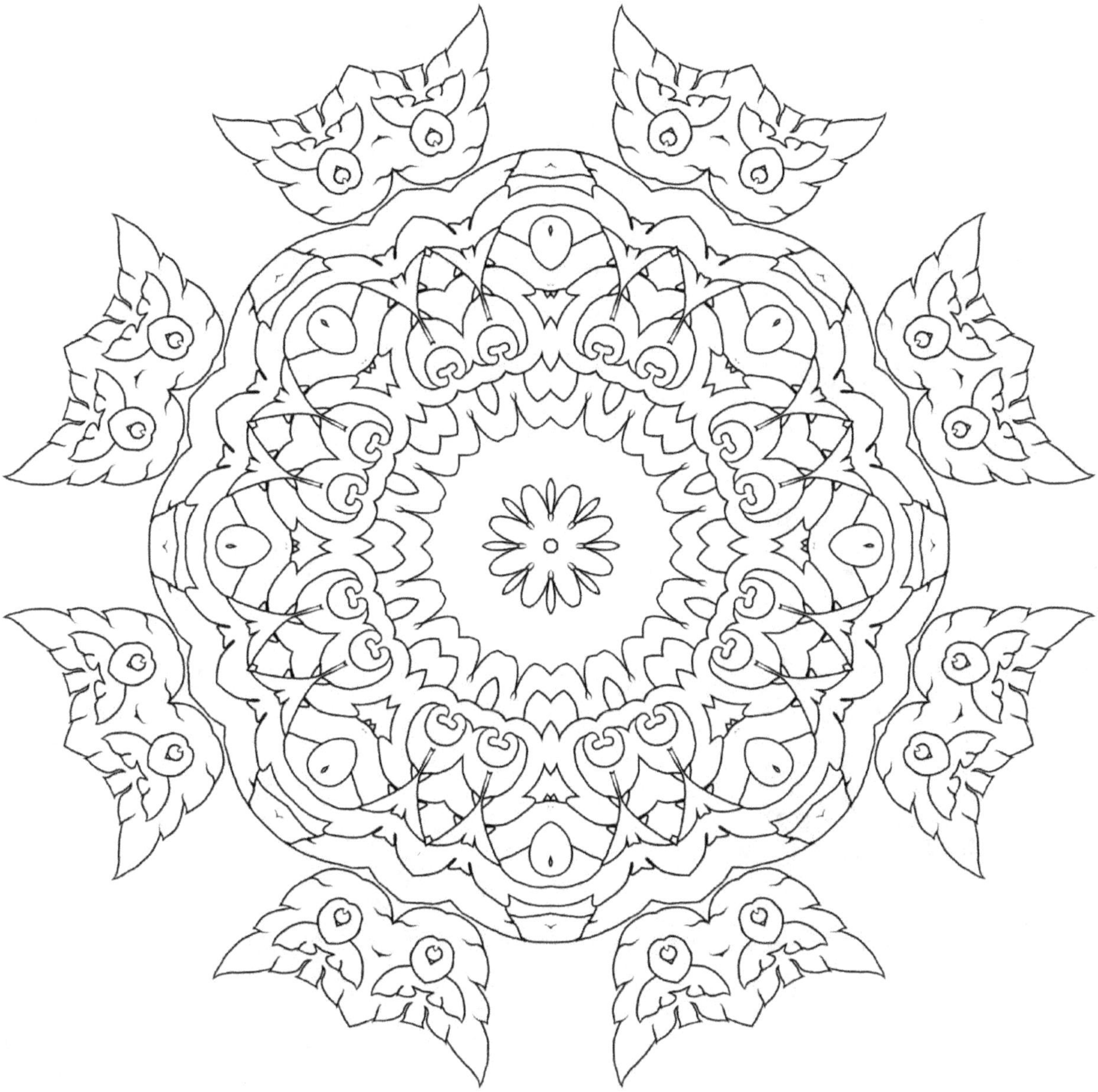

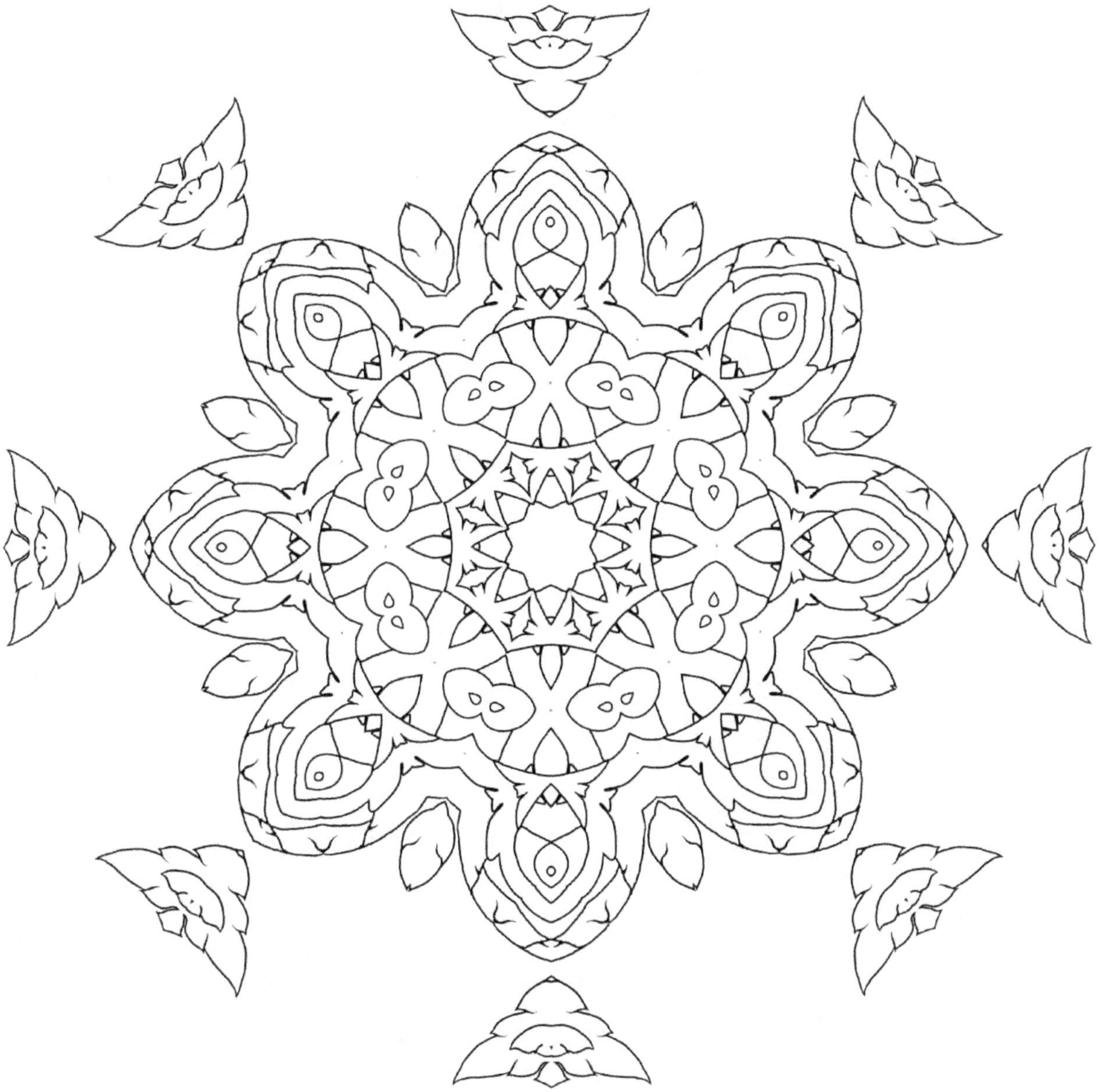

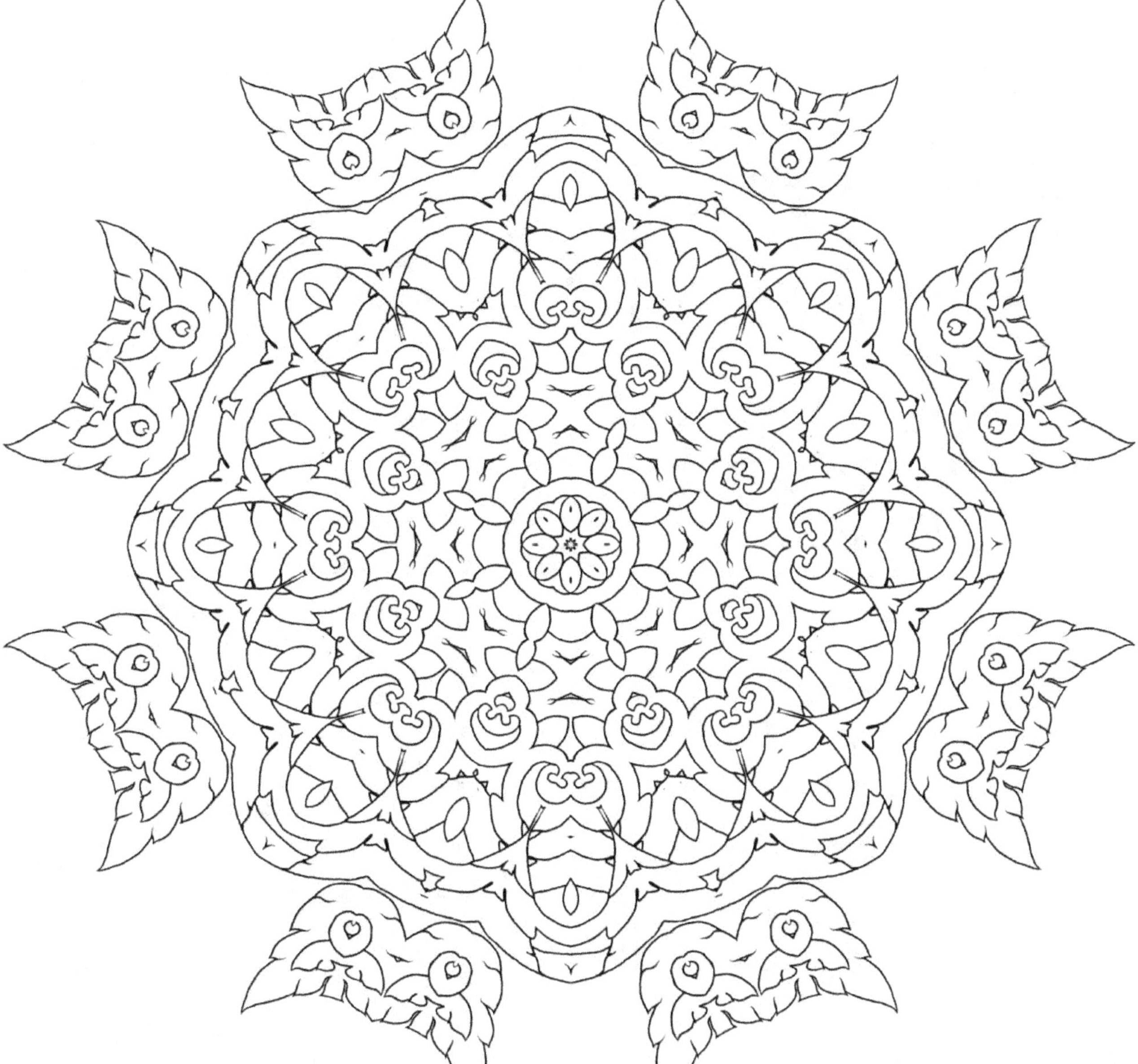

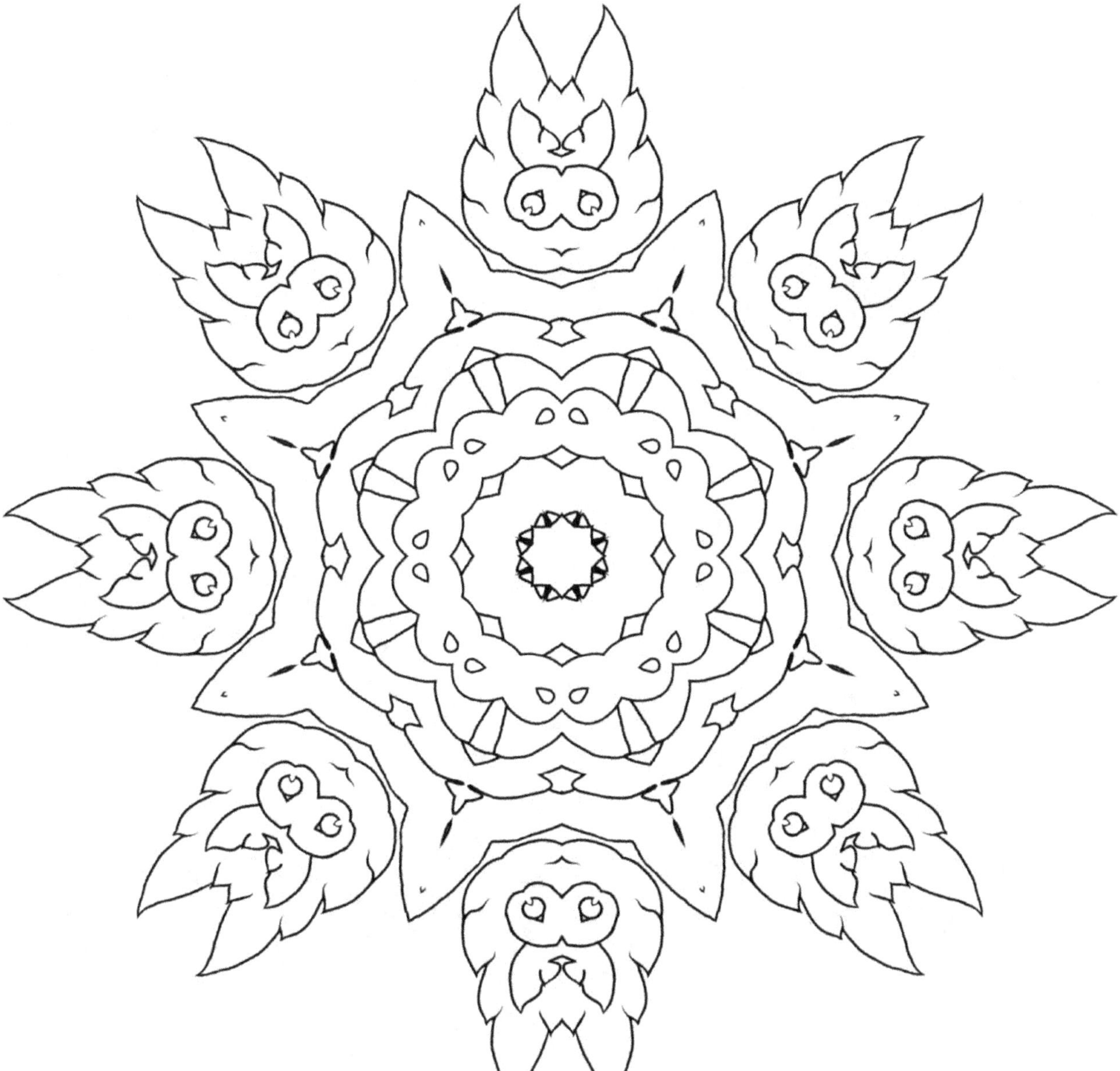

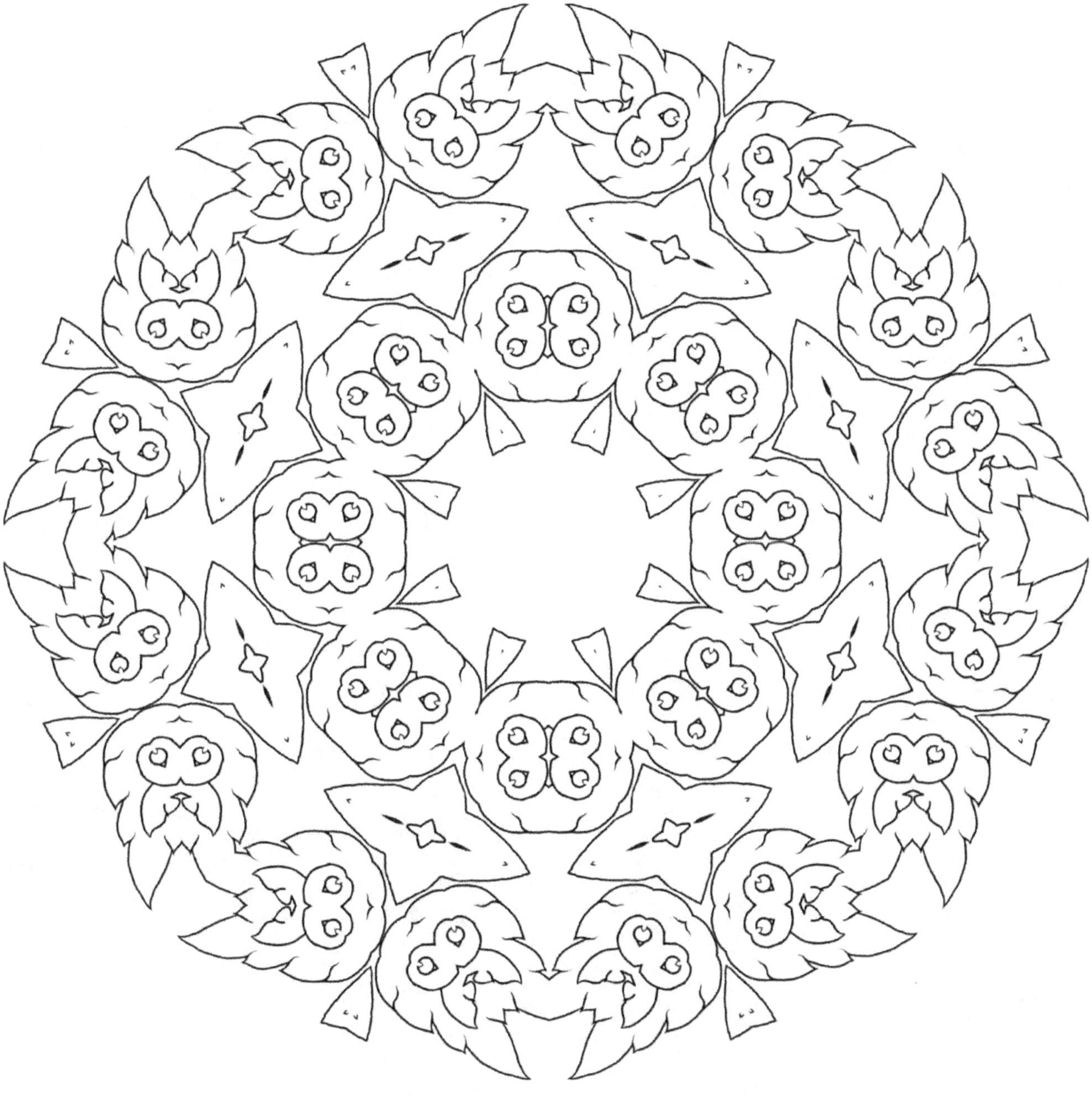

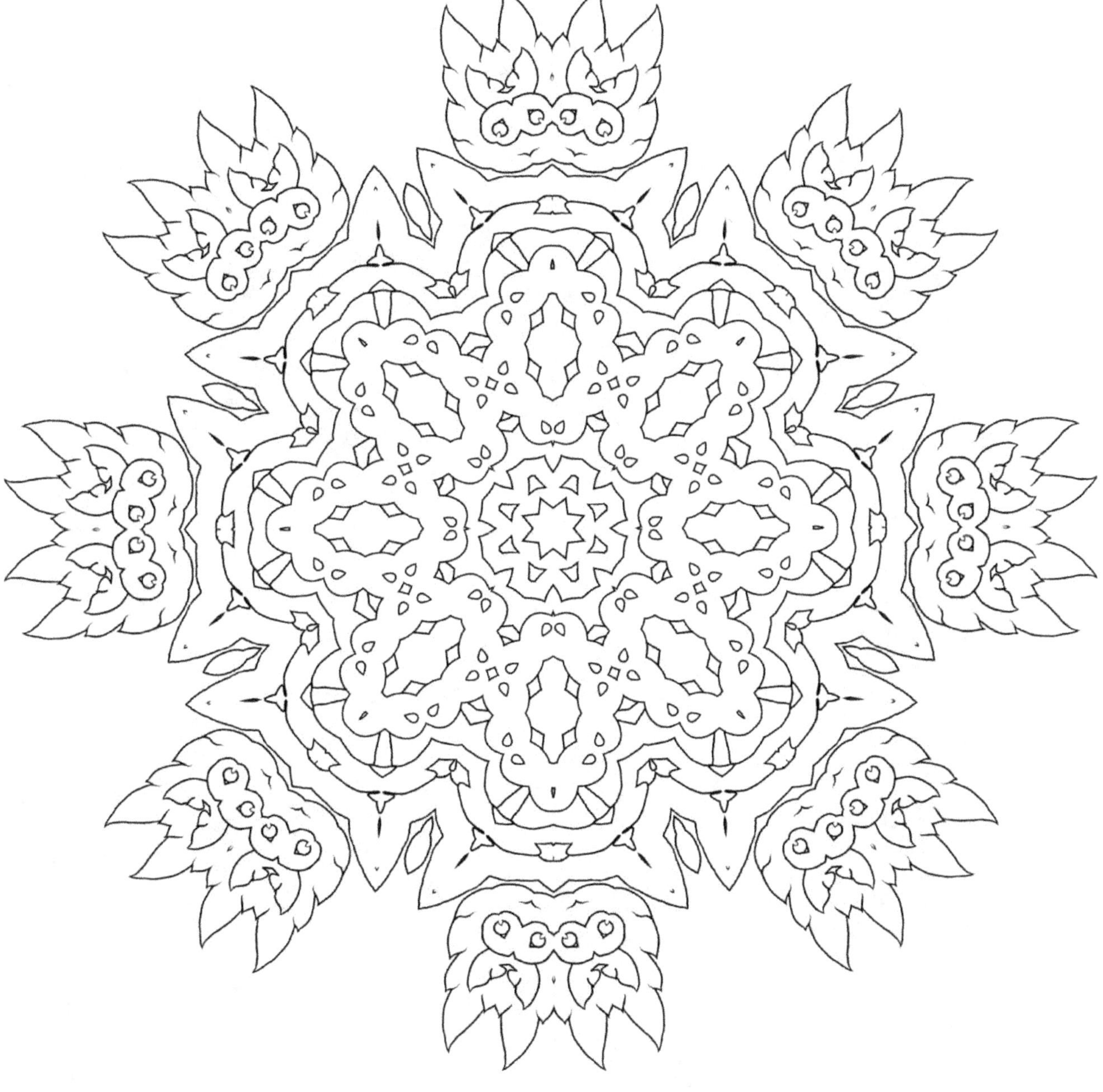

Thank you

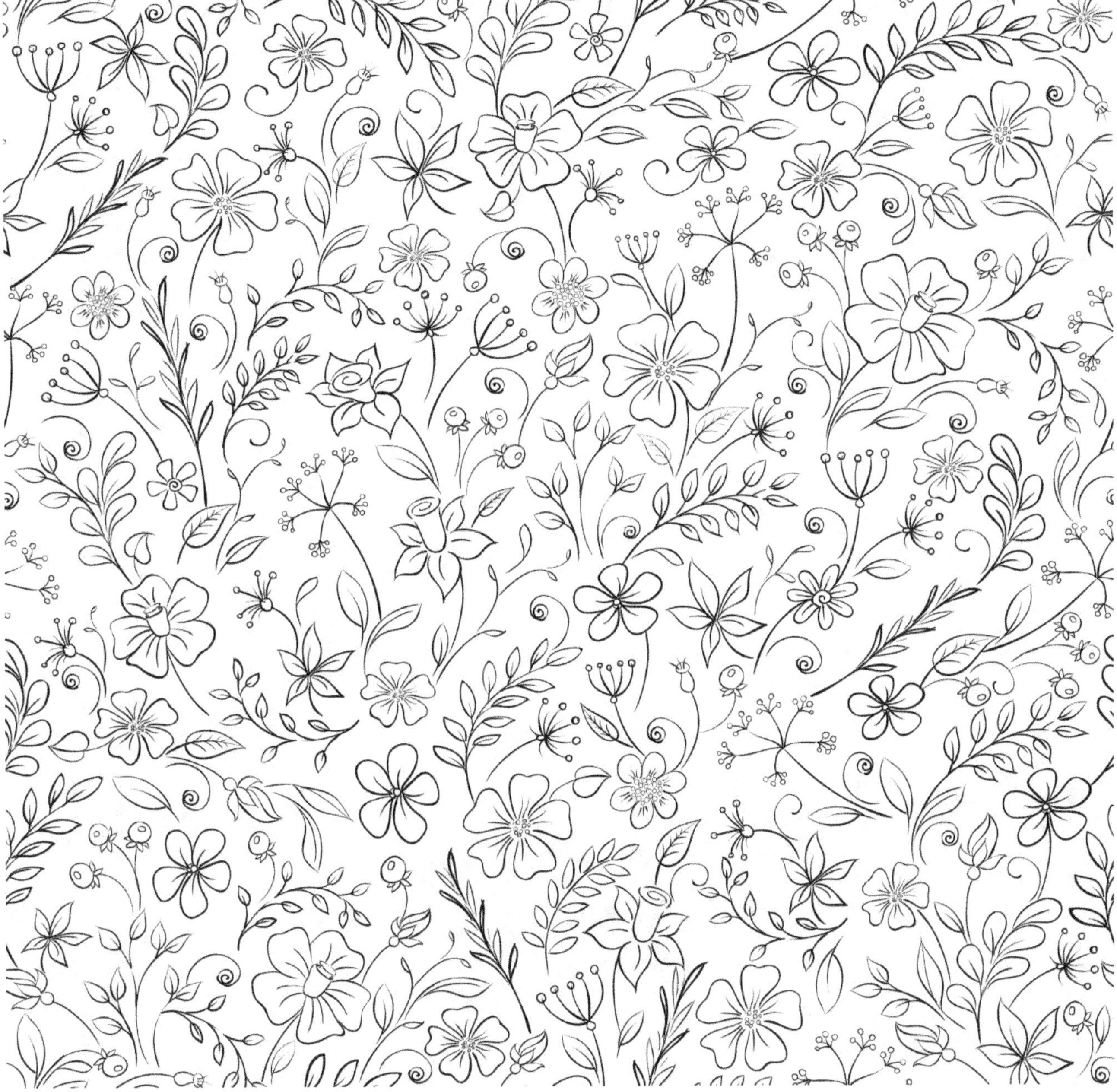

www.ingramcontent.com/pod-product-compliance
Lightning Source LLC
Chambersburg PA
CBHW081117180526
45170CB00008B/2884
* 9 7 8 1 5 4 2 6 3 0 2 0 7 *